Yuletide Essentials

Yuletide Essentials

Matthew Petchinsky

Yuletide Essentials: A Complete Guide to an Authentic and Magical Christmas

By: Matthew Petchinsky

Chapter 1: Embracing the Spirit of the Season
Introduction to Christmas as a Time for Love, Unity, and Gratitude

Christmas is much more than a day marked by gifts and glittering lights; it is an echo of timeless stories and age-old traditions that speak to the human spirit. At its heart, Christmas is a time to pause, reflect, and immerse oneself in the richness of love, unity, and gratitude. This chapter invites you to step away from the rush of the holiday season and delve into the true essence of what makes this time of year so enchanting and transformative.

The Origin of Christmas Spirit

The spirit of Christmas has its roots in stories that span centuries. From tales of the birth of Christ celebrated in candlelit churches to the pagan festivals that honored the winter solstice, this season has always been about celebrating life, rebirth, and communal ties. While the historical underpinnings of Christmas are diverse, they converge on a singular theme: togetherness and hope.

Modern Christmas rituals have evolved, incorporating a rich tapestry of customs from around the world—feasting, singing carols, sharing gifts, and crafting festive decorations. Yet, beneath the surface of these traditions lies a more profound truth. Christmas is an invitation to nurture warmth within our hearts and share it with those around us, creating memories that last a lifetime.

Love: The Foundation of the Holiday

At its core, Christmas is a celebration of love—unconditional, boundless, and encompassing. Love is the silent driver behind the gifts exchanged, the meals shared, and the laughter that fills our homes. It is the love of family and friends that brings light during the darkest days of winter. This season reminds us that even the simplest gestures can reflect profound affection.

To embrace the spirit of love during Christmas, consider small acts of kindness. A handwritten note expressing your appreciation, a heartfelt conversation, or a surprise call to a distant friend can carry more significance than any gift wrapped in fancy paper. This love extends not just to those we know but also to strangers—through charity, volunteering, or sharing words of kindness.

Unity: Coming Together as One

One of the most beautiful aspects of Christmas is its ability to bring people together. It bridges generational gaps, unites cultures, and fosters a sense of community that is both palpable and profound. The season's magic lies in its power to weave a collective fabric of joy, whether it is shared around a roaring fire with family or during a community event that lights up the town square.

To truly feel the spirit of unity, create opportunities for shared experiences. Organize a family gathering where each member shares a memory or a story that captures their favorite Christmas moments. Participate in local festivities, like tree lighting ceremonies or charity drives, to feel connected to your community. This shared sense of belonging is a testament to the season's ability to erase the invisible walls that often separate us.

Gratitude: The Heart's Response

Gratitude is the foundation upon which joy is built, and during Christmas, it becomes an essential part of the celebration. When we take a moment to count our blessings, we shift our focus from what is missing to what is abundantly present in our lives. Gratitude enriches the soul, making each moment more meaningful and each memory more vivid.

To integrate gratitude into your holiday routine, start with simple practices. Create a gratitude journal where you note down what you're thankful for each day in December. Share this practice with loved ones by expressing out loud what you appreciate about each person gathered at the Christmas table. This reinforces bonds and reminds everyone that true happiness is found in shared appreciation.

Creating a Personal and Meaningful Christmas

Christmas should be as unique as the individuals celebrating it. Personalizing your holiday season goes beyond decking the halls or preparing elaborate feasts; it's about infusing traditions with your essence. Whether that means starting a new family tradition, revisiting long-forgotten ones, or simply spending the day in quiet reflection, the goal is to create a celebration that resonates with your soul.

Consider crafting handmade ornaments that tell a story of your year, curating a playlist of songs that spark joy, or creating a family photo book that spans the seasons of the past. Personal touches make Christmas unforgettable and deepen its meaning, transforming it from a date on the calendar into a cherished memory.

Final Thoughts: The Warmth of the Season

Christmas is, at its heart, a reminder of what we hold dear—love, unity, and gratitude. It is a time to extend a hand, share a smile, and cherish those around us. As you embark on this season, let it be filled with moments that speak to you, whether they are loud and boisterous or quiet and reflective. The spirit of Christmas is not found in the grandeur of the celebration but in the sincerity of the heart. Let this be the season that brings you closer to yourself and others, creating ripples of joy that last far beyond December.

Embrace the season, and let its spirit fill your days with warmth and wonder.

Chapter 2: Crafting Your Unique Holiday Rituals
Ideas for Establishing Family or Individual Traditions That Bring Lasting Memories

The beauty of Christmas is that it's not bound by a universal script. While classic traditions like decorating a tree or exchanging gifts are widespread, the real magic lies in the personal touches that make the holiday uniquely yours. Crafting your own holiday rituals can deepen your connection to the season, turn everyday moments into cherished memories, and offer continuity that families and individuals alike can look forward to year after year. This chapter provides a comprehensive guide on how to create meaningful, custom holiday traditions that will stand the test of time.

The Significance of Holiday Rituals

Rituals have a way of embedding themselves into our hearts. They provide comfort, structure, and a sense of belonging. During Christmas, rituals offer an opportunity to slow down and savor moments that might otherwise be lost in the rush of the season. Whether you're celebrating with family, friends, or alone, establishing your own holiday rituals can make the season deeply personal and emotionally enriching.

Building a Foundation for Your Traditions

The first step to creating unique holiday rituals is understanding what aspects of Christmas resonate most with you or your family. Do you cherish the togetherness, the creative aspects of decorating, or the moments of reflection and gratitude? Identifying these elements helps guide the types of traditions you might wish to establish.

Here are some key areas to consider when building your own holiday rituals:

1. **Decorating the Christmas Tree: A Centerpiece of Creativity**
   - *Personalized Ornaments*: Make or purchase ornaments that reflect meaningful events or interests. Each year, add a new ornament that represents a significant milestone or shared memory, turning your tree into a timeline of cherished moments.
   - *Family Decorating Night*: Dedicate a specific evening to decorating the tree together. Play holiday music, sip on hot chocolate, and share stories or memories as you place each ornament. This turns a simple task into an event that everyone anticipates.
   - *Themed Trees*: For families who love creativity, consider choosing a theme for your tree each year. Whether it's a favorite book series, a color scheme, or a historical period, themed trees can become a fun and evolving tradition.

2. **Unique Gift-Giving Ceremonies**
   - *Secret Santa with a Twist*: Instead of traditional Secret Santa, add challenges or themes to the gifts. For instance, gifts could be handmade or need to align with a specific interest of the recipient. This adds a layer of excitement and creativity.
   - *Gift Exchange Games*: Introduce games like "White Elephant" or a scavenger hunt where participants have to fol-

low clues to find their gifts. These playful activities turn gift-giving into a shared experience full of laughter and fun.

- *Letter-Wrapped Presents*: Attach a heartfelt letter to each gift explaining why you chose it. This small gesture enhances the sentimental value of the present and strengthens connections.

3. **Handcrafted Holiday Decorations**

- *DIY Advent Calendars*: Create your own advent calendar filled with personalized notes, small gifts, or activities for each day leading up to Christmas. This tradition builds anticipation and makes each day of December feel special.

- *Wreath-Making Workshops*: Host a family or friends' night dedicated to crafting holiday wreaths using natural materials, ribbons, and baubles. The finished wreaths can be hung on doors as a reminder of the shared experience.

- *Personalized Stockings*: Make or decorate stockings for each family member with unique elements that reflect their personalities or favorite interests.

4. **Storytelling and Memory Sharing**

- *Christmas Eve Storytelling*: On Christmas Eve, gather around to share stories. These could be traditional holiday tales, family anecdotes, or even imaginative stories that children make up on the spot. Storytelling brings warmth and laughter and strengthens the bonds between listeners.

- *Annual Christmas Journal*: Start a journal where everyone writes down their favorite memory from the season. Over the years, this journal will become a treasured keepsake filled with reflections and moments that encapsulate the essence of your holiday celebrations.

5. Cooking and Baking Traditions

- *Signature Family Dish*: Create a special dish or dessert that is only made during the holiday season. Whether it's a unique take on a Christmas pie or a special hot drink, this dish becomes a symbol of your shared time together.
- *Baking Day*: Dedicate a full day to baking cookies, cakes, and other holiday treats as a family or with friends. Distribute these goodies to neighbors, friends, or local charities to spread joy beyond your own home.
- *Recipe Exchange*: If celebrating with extended family or friends, organize a recipe exchange where everyone brings their favorite holiday dish and shares the recipe. This not only adds variety to your holiday meals but also builds a shared tradition that evolves with the tastes and experiences of your circle.

- **6.Acts of Kindness and Giving Back**
  - *Season of Service*: Commit to one day during the holiday season where your family or group volunteers at a local shelter, food bank, or community center. This tradition helps instill the true spirit of giving and gratitude in the youngest family members and deepens your own sense of purpose during the holidays.
  - *Anonymous Kindness Gifts*: Create a tradition of leaving small, anonymous gifts or cards for neighbors or community members who might be in need of a bit of extra holiday cheer.
  - *Charity Auction Night*: Host an auction where homemade crafts, baked goods, or donated items are

bid on, with proceeds going to a chosen charity. This fun and interactive event can be a great annual gathering that reinforces the importance of community and kindness.

- **7.Seasonal Crafts and Projects**
  - *Annual Ornament Craft*: Dedicate time each year to creating new holiday ornaments. Whether they're made from paper, clay, or natural materials, these ornaments can become a cherished part of your collection and a reminder of that year's celebration.
  - *Memory Garlands*: Create garlands with photos, notes, or small drawings that capture the past year's highlights. These garlands can be hung across doorways or mantels, bringing personal history into the festive decor.
  - *Winter Wonderland Scene*: Build a miniature village that grows a little each year. Add handcrafted or collected pieces annually to turn your home into a personalized winter wonderland.

Personalizing Your Rituals

The true magic of holiday traditions comes from how they evolve and adapt over time. What begins as a simple idea can become a beloved ritual that is eagerly anticipated year after year. The key to lasting traditions is to keep them flexible and open to change, allowing new experiences to be integrated as families grow and change.

Ask yourself or your family what moments were the most enjoyable and meaningful each year. Reflect on these moments and brainstorm ways to enhance or build on them for the following holiday season. This ensures your holiday rituals remain fresh, relevant, and filled with joy.

Final Thoughts: The Gift of Tradition

Creating your own holiday traditions is about fostering a deep connection to the season and the people around you. Whether you embrace a quiet evening of reflection, a bustling day of cooking and decorating, or an elaborate gift-giving ceremony, the essence lies in the joy and love shared. These rituals provide a sturdy framework on which holiday memories are built and cherished. Let this be the chapter of your holiday season that writes itself year after year, full of laughter, warmth, and the unique touches that make it yours.

Chapter 3: The Art of Sustainable and Natural Decor

Tips on Decorating with Sustainability in Mind Using Natural, Eco-Friendly Elements

In today's world, sustainability has become more than a passing trend; it's a mindful way of living that enriches our connection to the Earth. Christmas, with all its brightness and festivity, can sometimes lead to excessive consumption and waste. However, embracing eco-friendly and natural decorations allows us to celebrate the season while respecting the planet. This chapter delves into the art of sustainable holiday decor, focusing on creative ways to use natural elements like pine cones, dried fruit, and handmade ornaments to create a beautiful and environmentally conscious Christmas.

Why Choose Sustainable Decor?

Sustainable holiday decor emphasizes the use of renewable, biodegradable, or recycled materials to reduce the environmental impact of the season. By opting for eco-friendly decorations, you contribute to a healthier planet and create a more personal and heartwarming holiday atmosphere. Natural decor items often bring warmth and authenticity, making your holiday space feel more connected to nature and tradition.

Getting Started with Sustainable Decor

Before diving into specific decorating ideas, consider these essential tips to guide your sustainable decor journey:

1. **Use What You Have**: Start by assessing what you already own. Repurpose items from previous holidays and incorporate them into your new eco-friendly design. Upcycling old decorations not only saves money but also minimizes waste.

2. **Plan Ahead**: Sustainable decorating benefits from planning. Before collecting or purchasing materials, decide on a theme or color palette that fits your style. This helps you avoid impulsive buying and ensures a cohesive look.

3. **Focus on Quality Over Quantity**: Instead of overloading your home with decorations, choose fewer, high-quality pieces that have meaning or functionality.

Natural Elements for Sustainable Decor

1. Pine Cones Pine cones are abundant during the winter months and make versatile decoration pieces. They're perfect for adding rustic charm and are completely biodegradable.

- *Pine Cone Garlands*: String together pine cones using jute twine or cotton rope to create a beautiful, natural garland. Add sprigs of evergreen or berries for a touch of color.
- *Scented Pine Cones*: Infuse pine cones with essential oils like cinnamon or clove to add a subtle holiday fragrance to your home. Simply bake the pine cones at a low temperature to ensure they are clean and dry, then sprinkle a few drops of essential oil over them.
- *Pine Cone Centerpieces*: Arrange pine cones in a bowl or basket with other natural elements like acorns, dried leaves, and small branches to create a stunning, earthy centerpiece.

2. Dried Fruit Dried fruit, especially oranges, apples, and cranberries, is a popular option for sustainable holiday decor. Not only are they biodegradable, but they also add vibrant color and natural fragrance to your space.

- *Dried Orange Garland*: Slice oranges thinly, place them on a baking sheet, and dry them in the oven at a low temperature. Once dried, thread them onto a string or ribbon to create a garland that can be hung on the tree, across a mantel, or around door frames.
- *Fruit and Spice Ornaments*: Combine dried orange slices with cinnamon sticks, star anise, and cloves. These can be hung on the

tree or used as decorative accents on wrapped gifts for an added festive touch.

- *Dried Fruit Wreath*: Use a wire frame as a base and attach dried orange slices, apple rings, and cranberries using thin wire or glue. Enhance the wreath with sprigs of rosemary or eucalyptus for a splash of greenery and aroma.

3. Handmade Ornaments Handmade ornaments are not only environmentally friendly but also add a personalized touch to your holiday decor. Creating these with family or friends can become a cherished tradition.

- *Salt Dough Ornaments*: Mix flour, salt, and water to create salt dough. Roll out the dough, use cookie cutters to make festive shapes, and bake until hard. Once cooled, decorate with natural paints or leave them plain for a rustic look.
- *Wooden Ornaments*: Collect small, fallen branches and cut them into discs. Use wood-burning tools or eco-friendly markers to draw holiday symbols or write messages. Drill a small hole for threading twine and hang them on the tree.
- *Paper Decorations*: Use recycled paper or craft paper to create origami stars, snowflakes, or chains. This is an excellent way to repurpose old books or newspapers.

4. Greenery and Nature's Bounty Utilize the natural beauty of greenery, such as evergreen branches, holly, and mistletoe, to decorate your home with the essence of the season.

- *Evergreen Garlands*: Gather branches from pine, fir, or cedar and create garlands to hang over doorways or staircases. Secure the branches with twine or floral wire and weave in other elements like pine cones or ribbons made of natural fibers.

- *Mini Holiday Trees*: Collect branches and arrange them in a pot or vase to mimic a small Christmas tree. Decorate with handmade or natural ornaments for a simple, elegant look.
- *Fresh Centerpieces*: Combine sprigs of greenery with natural elements like cranberries, cinnamon sticks, and dried citrus in a bowl or wooden box to create a fragrant and eye-catching table centerpiece.

5. Sustainable Candles and Lighting Lighting sets the mood for the holiday season, but traditional lights can consume significant energy.

- *Soy or Beeswax Candles*: Choose candles made from natural soy or beeswax instead of paraffin. These are not only more sustainable but also cleaner burning and often come with natural scents.
- *Upcycled Jar Lanterns*: Use old glass jars to make lanterns. Fill them with dried cranberries, a bit of water, and floating tea lights for a festive, glowing effect.
- *Energy-Efficient LED Lights*: If you do use electric lights, opt for energy-efficient LED versions. Solar-powered string lights are another great option for outdoor decorations.

Tips for Collecting Natural Materials

- *Be Mindful*: When gathering materials like pine cones, acorns, or branches, ensure you do so responsibly and without disrupting local wildlife habitats.
- *Clean and Preserve*: Rinse any collected natural items and let them air dry before use. This helps remove dirt and potential pests.
- *Seasonal Storage*: Store decorations properly at the end of the season to extend their life. For example, keep dried fruit and greenery in airtight containers to prevent mold or pests.

Crafting with a Conscience

Creating sustainable holiday decor can be a rewarding experience that strengthens your connection to the season and the natural world. Whether you're upcycling items, crafting with found objects, or choosing biodegradable decorations, each effort contributes to a healthier planet. These traditions not only reduce waste but also teach future generations the importance of mindful living.

Embracing Minimalism and Nature's Aesthetic

The beauty of natural decor lies in its simplicity and elegance. By focusing on a minimalist approach, you can let the raw textures, colors, and scents of nature take center stage. This can create a calming and serene holiday environment, contrasting with the more commercial and cluttered aesthetics commonly seen.

Final Thoughts: Creating Beauty with Intention

The true spirit of sustainable holiday decorating lies in the joy of creation, the connection to nature, and the memories formed along the way. By incorporating natural and eco-friendly elements into your holiday decor, you not only celebrate the season with love and warmth but also nurture the world around you. Let this Christmas be a testament to your creativity, care, and commitment to a more sustainable future.

Chapter 4: A Warm Welcome – Creating an Inviting Home for the Holidays

Techniques for Transforming Every Room into a Cozy, Festive Haven, with Emphasis on the Kitchen and Living Room as Gathering Spaces

The holiday season is a time when homes come alive with warmth, laughter, and the joy of loved ones gathering together. Creating an inviting atmosphere is not just about hanging decorations or stringing up lights—it's about cultivating a space that makes people feel welcomed and cherished. This chapter delves into detailed techniques for transforming every room into a cozy, festive haven, with special focus on the kitchen and living room, the heart of holiday gatherings.

The Essence of a Cozy, Festive Home

A warm, inviting home for the holidays is a combination of sensory experiences: the glow of soft lights, the scent of baked goods and pine, the touch of plush fabrics, and the sight of meaningful decorations. Thoughtful design and decoration turn your living space into a comforting embrace that beckons guests to stay and enjoy.

Creating Ambiance in Every Room

1. The Living Room: The Heart of Festivity The living room is often the first space guests see and the main hub for holiday activities, from opening presents to storytelling by the fire.

- *Centerpiece – The Christmas Tree*: Start with a tree that matches the scale of your space. Decorate it using a cohesive color scheme or mix sentimental and homemade ornaments for a personalized touch. To add depth, layer different types of decorations: garlands, ornaments, and small lights. Place a tree skirt or decorative blanket around the base for an added touch of warmth.
- *Layered Lighting*: Create a welcoming glow using a combination of light sources. Incorporate fairy lights, string lights along the

mantel, and place LED candles on side tables. For a more rustic look, consider lanterns with battery-operated candles that mimic a real flame.

- *Cozy Textiles*: Drape blankets and throw pillows in festive fabrics across sofas and chairs. Look for materials such as faux fur, knit, or velvet in holiday colors like deep red, forest green, or ivory. Layering different textures will give your space a rich, inviting feel.
- *Seasonal Scents*: Infuse the living room with seasonal scents using essential oil diffusers or natural potpourri. Simmer pots filled with cinnamon sticks, orange slices, cloves, and cranberries create a warm, inviting fragrance.
- *Decorative Touches*: Add small, meaningful decorations such as nutcracker figurines, a bowl of pine cones, or framed holiday art. Hanging stockings over the mantel or on a decorative ladder can also elevate the festive feel.

2. The Kitchen: The Heart of Holiday Cheer The kitchen is more than just a place to cook; it's where stories are shared, recipes come to life, and the warmth of the season is most tangibly felt.

- *Festive Baking Station*: Dedicate a part of your counter or island to a holiday baking station, complete with jars of flour, sugar, cocoa, and holiday-themed sprinkles. Add a decorative jar of wooden spoons or spatulas with festive prints.
- *Holiday Linens*: Replace everyday towels and table linens with ones featuring holiday motifs or colors. A holiday-themed table runner or placemats can create a cohesive look.
- *Scented Enhancements*: Keep cinnamon sticks, vanilla pods, and cloves in small decorative jars for quick access while baking. These natural scents will infuse the space with a holiday aroma that makes the kitchen feel warm and inviting.
- *Open Shelving and Displays*: If your kitchen has open shelves, decorate them with garlands, miniature wreaths, or festive dish-

ware. Place holiday mugs and seasonal spices within reach to encourage guests to make their own warm drinks, like hot chocolate or mulled cider.

- *Mood Lighting*: Use under-cabinet lights or battery-operated candles to add a soft glow to the kitchen. This keeps the space cozy, even after cooking is done.

3. Dining Room: Setting the Stage for Festive Meals The dining room is where loved ones gather for meals, making it a place where comfort and festivity are essential.

- *Tablescaping*: Create a centerpiece using a mix of greenery, candles, and ornaments. Use a table runner made from burlap or a fabric with holiday patterns for a rustic touch. Scatter pinecones or faux snow for added detail.
- *Chair Decorations*: Tie bows or place mini wreaths on the backs of chairs for an elegant touch. Use ribbon in holiday colors or natural twine for a more rustic look.
- *Place Settings*: Elevate the table by layering plates with chargers, adding folded cloth napkins with a sprig of rosemary or holly tucked inside. Personalized name cards or small holiday trinkets at each setting add a special touch.

4. Bedrooms: A Cozy Retreat Bringing the holiday spirit to bedrooms can create an all-encompassing atmosphere of warmth throughout the house.

- *Festive Bedding*: Switch out everyday bedding for sheets and duvets in holiday colors or patterns, such as plaid or snowflake designs. Add throw pillows and blankets for extra coziness.
- *Subtle Decor*: Place small decorative touches like miniature Christmas trees, garlands, or string lights around headboards or window frames.

- *Scented Sachets*: Place holiday-scented sachets in closets or under pillows to maintain a festive scent in the room.

5. Entryway: A Warm Welcome The entryway sets the tone for your entire home and should be welcoming and festive.

- *Seasonal Wreaths*: Hang a wreath made of fresh greenery, pinecones, or dried citrus slices on the front door. If possible, add battery-operated lights or ribbon for extra flair.
- *Console Table Decor*: Adorn your entryway table with a bowl of pinecones, a small vase of winter greenery, and a few candles. Place a mirror above the table with a garland draped over the top to reflect light and make the space feel larger.
- *Welcome Mats*: Use a holiday-themed welcome mat to set a cheerful tone as soon as guests arrive.

Personalizing Your Decor

The most memorable homes are those that reflect the personalities of the people who live in them. Incorporate family heirlooms, crafts, or photos that tell a story. Displaying holiday cards from friends and family on a string across the mantel or on a pinboard adds a layer of warmth and personal connection.

DIY Ideas for Extra Coziness

- *Handmade Ornaments*: Get creative with your family by making ornaments out of salt dough, felt, or recycled materials. This can be a fun activity for children and adults alike, and each ornament can carry a memory.
- *Personalized Stockings*: Decorate plain stockings with fabric paint, iron-on designs, or embroidery that represents each family member.

- *Photo Garland*: Create a garland of family holiday photos from past years. This is a great conversation starter and a way to reminisce on shared memories.

Finishing Touches: The Small Details that Matter

- *Music*: Soft holiday music playing in the background can make any space feel more festive. Curate a playlist that suits your family's tastes, ranging from classic carols to modern holiday hits.
- *Seasonal Drinks Station*: Set up a self-serve hot cocoa or mulled cider station in the living room or kitchen with holiday mugs, candy canes, cinnamon sticks, and whipped cream.
- *Fresh Flowers*: Use poinsettias, amaryllis, or even simple greenery in vases to add color and life to your rooms.

Final Thoughts: Embracing the Warmth of the Season

Transforming your home into a festive haven is about more than just decoration; it's about creating an atmosphere where memories can be made and cherished. Each space in your home offers a unique opportunity to spread holiday cheer, from the living room where stories unfold by the fire to the kitchen that hums with the warmth of baked treats and laughter. By paying attention to the details and infusing each room with a mix of natural, personal, and sustainable elements, you create a holiday environment that wraps everyone who enters in comfort and joy.

Chapter 5: Curating the Perfect Christmas Music Playlist Suggestions for Creating Playlists That Capture the Holiday Spirit, Mixing Traditional Carols with Contemporary Favorites

Music has an unparalleled ability to evoke memories, set moods, and transport us to places of comfort and joy. During the holiday season, the right music can transform a room, enrich festive gatherings, and offer a backdrop to quiet, contemplative moments by the fire. Crafting the perfect Christmas playlist is an art form, blending nostalgia, tradition, and modern flair to create a balanced listening experience. This chapter delves into how to create the ultimate Christmas playlist that embodies the spirit of the season, whether you're hosting a lively party, enjoying a cozy evening at home, or setting the mood for holiday cooking.

The Role of Music in Enhancing the Holiday Experience

Christmas music is more than just background noise; it's the soundtrack to the season's most cherished moments. From the soulful notes of a classic carol to the upbeat rhythm of a modern holiday hit, the songs we choose to play shape our holiday experiences and anchor memories. Crafting a playlist with variety and flow ensures that your holiday gatherings, family traditions, and personal moments are wrapped in an ambiance that reflects the magic of the season.

Building the Foundation: Categories of Holiday Music

To create a well-rounded playlist, it's helpful to understand the different types of Christmas songs available. A good playlist strikes a balance between these categories:

1. **Traditional Carols**: Timeless and rich in history, traditional carols are the backbone of any Christmas playlist. Songs like *"O Holy Night," "Silent Night,"* and *"Hark! The Herald Angels Sing"* bring a touch of solemnity and reverence to the season.

2. **Classic Christmas Hits**: These are the songs that everyone knows and loves, providing a sense of nostalgia. Think *"White Christmas"* by Bing Crosby, *"The Christmas Song (Chestnuts Roasting on an Open Fire)"* by Nat King Cole, and *"Rockin' Around the Christmas Tree"* by Brenda Lee.

3. **Contemporary Holiday Favorites**: Modern artists have contributed their own interpretations of Christmas songs and original compositions. *"All I Want for Christmas Is You"* by Mariah Carey, *"Underneath the Tree"* by Kelly Clarkson, and *"Last Christmas"* by Wham! are examples of songs that add a contemporary touch.

4. **Instrumental and Orchestral**: For a more subtle and elegant atmosphere, instrumental versions of popular carols and orchestral holiday music are perfect. Pieces by the Trans-Siberian Orchestra or the Nutcracker Suite by Tchaikovsky offer sophistication.

5. **Jazz and Blues Christmas**: Songs by artists like Ella Fitzgerald, Louis Armstrong, and Ray Charles lend a cozy, laid-back feel to your playlist. *"Have Yourself a Merry Little Christmas"* sung in a smooth, jazzy style can evoke warmth and nostalgia.

6. **Children's Christmas Songs**: If children are part of your holiday experience, including songs like *"Rudolph the Red-Nosed Reindeer"* and *"Frosty the Snowman"* ensures they can sing along and feel the holiday spirit.

7. **International Christmas Songs**: Don't forget to add songs from different cultures to bring a global touch to your playlist. Tracks like *"Feliz Navidad"* by José Feliciano and traditional French carols like *"Petit Papa Noël"* can introduce variety.

Curating a Balanced Playlist

When crafting a playlist, aim for a mix that seamlessly transitions between different types of songs. Here's how to structure your playlist to maintain interest and flow:

- **Start with the Classics**: Begin with well-known traditional or classic songs to set the holiday mood. This primes listeners for the nostalgia of the season.
- **Introduce Modern Hits**: Transition into contemporary songs to pick up the energy. These tracks will keep the playlist lively and engaging.
- **Add Instrumentals Midway**: Insert instrumental pieces or orchestral versions halfway through your playlist to create a calming break and allow people to chat, eat, or unwind.
- **Bring in the Jazz and Blues**: Follow up with a few jazz or blues tracks to create a cozy, intimate atmosphere.
- **Include Children's Songs if Applicable**: If your gathering includes kids, now is a good time to add some fun, sing-along songs.
- **End with Soulful and Sentimental Songs**: Close your playlist with slower, heartfelt tracks like *"O Holy Night"* or *"Have Yourself a Merry Little Christmas"* to leave everyone in a reflective, warm state.

Top Picks for Each Category
Traditional Carols:

- *"O Come, All Ye Faithful"* – Traditional Choirs
- *"Hark! The Herald Angels Sing"* – King's College Choir
- *"Silent Night"* – Bing Crosby or Josh Groban

Classic Christmas Hits:

- *"White Christmas"* – Bing Crosby
- *"The Christmas Song (Chestnuts Roasting on an Open Fire)"* – Nat King Cole
- *"It's the Most Wonderful Time of the Year"* – Andy Williams

Contemporary Holiday Favorites:

- *"All I Want for Christmas Is You"* – Mariah Carey
- *"Underneath the Tree"* – Kelly Clarkson
- *"Last Christmas"* – Wham!

Instrumental and Orchestral:

- *"Christmas Eve/Sarajevo 12/24"* – Trans-Siberian Orchestra
- *"Dance of the Sugar Plum Fairy"* – Tchaikovsky
- *"Carol of the Bells"* – Piano Guys

Jazz and Blues Christmas:

- *"Let It Snow! Let It Snow! Let It Snow!"* – Ella Fitzgerald
- *"Merry Christmas Baby"* – Otis Redding
- *"What Are You Doing New Year's Eve?"* – Louis Armstrong

Children's Christmas Songs:

- *"Rudolph the Red-Nosed Reindeer"* – Gene Autry
- *"Frosty the Snowman"* – Jimmy Durante
- *"Jingle Bells"* – Various Artists

International Christmas Songs:

- *"Feliz Navidad"* – José Feliciano
- *"Petit Papa Noël"* – Tino Rossi
- *"O Tannenbaum"* – German Choirs

Personalizing Your Playlist

To make your playlist truly unique, incorporate songs that hold special meaning to you and your family. This could include tracks that remind you of childhood Christmases, songs that were played during important holiday moments, or even tunes that represent new memories you wish to create.

- **Holiday Memories**: Add songs that remind you of past holidays, like your favorite childhood carol or the first song played at a memorable Christmas party.
- **Family and Friend Favorites**: Ask family members or friends for their favorite holiday songs and include them in your playlist. This ensures everyone feels represented and connected.
- **Hidden Gems**: Discover lesser-known holiday tracks or versions of popular songs that bring a fresh sound to your playlist.

Playlist Tips for Specific Occasions

- **Holiday Party**: Create an upbeat, lively playlist with a mix of classic and contemporary hits. Keep the tempo varied to maintain energy but add occasional slower songs for balance.
- **Christmas Morning**: For gift-opening, opt for a playlist that begins with softer, traditional carols and gradually picks up tempo. This allows for a calm start while building excitement as the morning progresses.
- **Quiet Evenings**: For relaxed evenings by the fire, create a playlist heavy on instrumentals, jazz, and orchestral pieces with a sprinkling of slower carols.
- **Holiday Baking and Cooking**: Choose a mix of classic hits and fun, sing-along contemporary songs to keep the energy up and the mood light while working in the kitchen.

Creating Different Playlists for Different Moods

While it's important to have an all-purpose holiday playlist, creating separate playlists for different activities or moods can enhance each part of your holiday experience. Here are some ideas:

- *"Christmas Classics"* for an all-encompassing holiday feel
- *"Cozy Christmas Nights"* featuring soft carols and instrumentals
- *"Christmas Jazz Lounge"* with jazz and blues tracks
- *"Upbeat Holiday Party"* full of danceable, lively songs
- *"Children's Christmas Wonderland"* packed with fun, kid-friendly tracks

The Role of Streaming Services and Tools

Take advantage of streaming services like Spotify, Apple Music, and YouTube, which allow you to create and share playlists easily. Many of these platforms offer pre-made holiday playlists that can serve as inspiration or be customized to fit your needs. Use playlist tools to crossfade songs, adjust playback order, or find related tracks to keep your playlist diverse and engaging.

Final Thoughts: The Soundtrack to Your Holiday Memories

Curating the perfect Christmas playlist is about more than just finding the right songs—it's about creating an experience that resonates with your memories, traditions, and holiday spirit. Whether your playlist is filled with timeless carols, contemporary hits, or hidden gems, the right mix can become the soundtrack to some of your most treasured holiday moments. Let this be the season where music fills your home and your heart, crafting an auditory backdrop that echoes the joy, peace, and warmth of Christmas.

Chapter 6: Planning Your Christmas Eve and Christmas Day Activities

Engaging Ideas for Christmas Eve Rituals, Christmas Day Games, and Activities That Keep the Whole Family Involved

The magic of Christmas is often felt most strongly on Christmas Eve and Christmas Day, when loved ones gather together to celebrate traditions, share laughter, and create lasting memories. Planning a mix of activities that honor cherished customs while introducing new, exciting elements can make these days unforgettable. This chapter provides an extensive guide to planning Christmas Eve and Christmas Day activities that will engage everyone—from young children to adults—in the joy of the season.

Christmas Eve: Setting the Stage for Holiday Magic

Christmas Eve is filled with anticipation and a sense of enchantment. It's a time to reflect, come together, and prepare for the celebrations ahead. Creating intentional rituals for Christmas Eve builds anticipation and helps everyone feel connected to the deeper meaning of the season.

1. Christmas Eve Traditions and Rituals
Family Dinner and Recipe Traditions

- *Feast of Favorites*: Plan a dinner with traditional family recipes or holiday favorites that everyone looks forward to each year. You might include special dishes that are only served on Christmas Eve, making it a truly unique meal.
- *Cultural Dishes*: If your family has cultural or heritage-based dishes, Christmas Eve is a great time to celebrate these roots. Sharing recipes from different family backgrounds can lead to storytelling and teach children about their ancestry.

Christmas Eve Storytelling

- *Reading Holiday Classics*: Gather everyone in a cozy space and read classic Christmas tales such as *"The Night Before Christmas"* or *"A Christmas Carol."* This is a quiet, reflective activity that sets a calm and magical tone for the night.
- *Family Memories*: Invite family members to share their favorite Christmas memories or traditions. This activity connects generations and allows everyone to reminisce, laugh, and feel gratitude for the holiday season.

Holiday Pajama Exchange

- *Matching Pajamas*: Gift everyone matching holiday pajamas on Christmas Eve. This playful ritual is perfect for photos and adds an extra layer of excitement as everyone gets cozy for the night.
- *Pajama Gift Wrapping*: For a twist, hide the pajamas around the house and send each family member on a mini scavenger hunt to find their pair. The hunt brings added fun and laughter to the evening.

Santa Preparation Rituals

- *Cookies and Milk*: Let children help bake and decorate cookies for Santa. Place them on a special plate with a glass of milk, creating a moment of excitement and wonder.
- *Reindeer Food*: Make a batch of "reindeer food" (oats mixed with glitter or edible sprinkles) for kids to sprinkle outside. This small tradition adds magic to the night and gives children a sense of participation in the holiday.
- *Letters to Santa*: For younger children, consider writing letters to Santa on Christmas Eve, summarizing the year's events or express-

ing gratitude. This can be a quiet moment for children to reflect on the holiday's meaning.

Christmas Eve Light Tour

- *Neighborhood Lights Tour*: Pile everyone into the car with blankets, hot cocoa, and holiday music, then drive around to see the neighborhood lights. This tradition can spark conversation, laughter, and admiration for the creativity and beauty of holiday decorations.
- *Candlelight Walk*: If you prefer a more reflective activity, take a candlelight walk around the neighborhood or yard. Sing carols or share holiday memories along the way for a tranquil, bonding experience.

2. Christmas Eve Games and Activities

Christmas Eve Bingo Create a Christmas-themed bingo game with holiday symbols like a snowman, Santa hat, Christmas tree, and bells. Use small prizes like candy canes, holiday stickers, or ornaments for winners.

Holiday Movie Marathon

- *Classic and Contemporary Mix*: Prepare a lineup of holiday classics (like *It's a Wonderful Life* or *A Charlie Brown Christmas*) mixed with newer family favorites (like *Elf* or *The Polar Express*). Offer popcorn, hot cocoa, and holiday cookies for a cozy movie night.
- *Interactive Movie Night*: Make the movie marathon interactive by incorporating small activities for each movie, like decorating cookies while watching *Home Alone* or doing a hot chocolate toast during *The Polar Express*.

Christmas Eve Slumber Party

- *Storytelling and Campfire*: Set up a small "campfire" with fairy lights or candles and share Christmas stories or folktales.
- *Holiday Karaoke*: Set up a karaoke machine or simply use YouTube and take turns singing favorite holiday songs. This lively activity adds humor and creates laughter-filled memories.

Christmas Day: Celebrating with Joy and Laughter

On Christmas Day, the excitement reaches its peak. Whether you enjoy a slow, leisurely morning or a bustling day full of activities, planning a mix of games and traditions will keep everyone engaged and connected.

1. Christmas Morning Traditions
Gift Opening Ceremonies

- *Themed Gift Opening*: Open gifts in themed rounds, such as "smallest gifts first," "gifts in a certain color," or "oldest to youngest." This makes gift-opening more fun and creates a sense of suspense.
- *Gift Thank-You Exchange*: After each gift is opened, have each recipient say something they're grateful for about the giver or share why they appreciate the gift. This practice fosters gratitude and appreciation.

Christmas Brunch

- *Family-Style Brunch*: Prepare a delicious brunch with everyone's favorite holiday treats, such as pancakes, cinnamon rolls, quiches, and seasonal fruits. Serve fresh-squeezed orange juice, coffee, and hot cocoa.

- *Make-Your-Own Waffle or Pancake Bar*: Set up a pancake or waffle station with toppings like fresh berries, whipped cream, chocolate chips, and syrup. This interactive breakfast is a hit with kids and adults alike.

2. Christmas Day Games and Activities
Holiday Charades

- *Christmas-Themed Prompts*: Create charades prompts with holiday themes like "wrapping a present," "singing carols," "building a snowman," or "decorating a tree." This game is easy to play, requires no materials, and guarantees laughter.
- *Team Challenge*: Divide into teams, and keep score for added excitement. Use holiday-themed prizes for the winning team, like festive cookies or homemade ornaments.

Gift Scavenger Hunt

- *Hidden Surprises*: Hide small gifts or stocking stuffers around the house and create a list of clues leading to each item. This is a fun activity that adds excitement, especially for kids.
- *Themed Hunts*: Tailor the scavenger hunt to the group, such as using riddles for older children or color-coded clues for younger ones.

Christmas Trivia

- *Holiday History*: Write down trivia questions about Christmas traditions, carols, and holiday history. Test everyone's knowledge with questions like "In which country did the Christmas tree tradition originate?" or "Which reindeer's name starts with a 'V'?"

- *Pop Culture Twist*: Include questions about famous holiday movies, songs, or books to appeal to various ages. Award small prizes to those who answer the most questions correctly.

Christmas Day Bingo Create a bingo card filled with Christmas Day activities, such as "eating cookies," "taking a family photo," "singing a carol," or "giving a hug." Family members mark off each square as they complete it, and the first one to get a bingo wins a prize.

Holiday Baking and Decorating

- *Cookie Decorating Competition*: Divide into teams and hold a cookie decorating contest. Provide various decorations, like icing, sprinkles, and edible glitter, and set a theme or let each team create their own design.
- *Gingerbread House Competition*: Host a gingerbread house-building competition with kits or homemade materials. Have a "judge" (or take a family vote) to determine the winner, or give awards for categories like "most creative" or "most festive."

Outdoor Activities for a White Christmas

- *Snowman-Building Contest*: If you have snow, organize a snowman-building contest and let everyone vote on their favorite creation.
- *Snowball Fight or Sledding*: Bundle up and head outdoors for a family snowball fight or sledding adventure. This is a great way to burn off energy and make the most of winter weather.
- *Winter Nature Walk*: For a quieter outdoor option, take a nature walk and enjoy the winter landscape. Bring hot chocolate in thermoses and point out winter birds or other wildlife.

3. Evening Activities to Wind Down Christmas Day

Family Christmas Movie Night Select a holiday classic that the entire family can enjoy to wind down after a busy day. Make it special by serving popcorn, holiday treats, and warm blankets for everyone to cuddle up with.

Christmas Day Reflection and Gratitude

- *Gratitude Jar*: Create a gratitude jar where each person writes down one thing they're grateful for that happened during the day. These notes can be kept and read aloud next year.
- *Family Storytelling*: Gather around the fire or in a cozy spot and share stories from the day. Reflect on favorite moments, express gratitude, and end the day on a warm note.

Christmas Karaoke Finale End the evening with a round of holiday karaoke. Let everyone choose a favorite song to sing, or perform duets and group songs to create a joyful close to the festivities.

Final Thoughts: Making Memories That Last

Planning engaging activities for Christmas Eve and Christmas Day ensures that the season's joy extends beyond gift-giving. These traditions, games, and moments of connection create memories that last a lifetime, bonding family and friends through laughter, gratitude, and shared experience. Embrace the joy and wonder of the season by incorporating rituals that speak to the heart, making each holiday special and unique.

Chapter 7: A Feast to Remember – Recipes for an Unforgettable Christmas Dinner

Unique, Easy-to-Follow Recipes That Focus on Both Tradition and New Culinary Twists

The heart of Christmas dinner is more than just a meal—it's a gathering filled with warmth, laughter, and stories shared over plates of delicious food. Crafting a Christmas feast that honors tradition while introducing fresh, exciting flavors can elevate your holiday dining experience and make it truly unforgettable. This chapter offers an array of recipes that combine classic holiday staples with modern, inventive twists to delight your guests and simplify your preparation.

Setting the Scene for Your Christmas Feast

Before diving into the recipes, consider the ambiance of your holiday table. A beautifully set table with festive decor enhances the dining experience. Incorporate elements like evergreen sprigs, candles, and elegant place settings to create an inviting and celebratory atmosphere. Now, onto the dishes that will make your Christmas dinner an event to remember.

Starters and Appetizers: The Prelude to the Feast
1. Baked Brie with Cranberry-Pecan Topping *Ingredients*:

- 1 wheel of brie cheese
- 1/2 cup fresh or frozen cranberries
- 1/4 cup chopped pecans
- 2 tbsp brown sugar
- 1 tbsp maple syrup
- Puff pastry (optional)
- Crackers or sliced baguette for serving

Instructions:

1. Preheat the oven to 375°F (190°C).
2. Place the brie on a parchment-lined baking sheet. If using puff pastry, wrap the brie and seal the edges.
3. In a saucepan, combine cranberries, brown sugar, maple syrup, and pecans. Cook over medium heat until the cranberries burst and the mixture thickens.
4. Spoon the cranberry-pecan mixture over the brie.
5. Bake for 10-12 minutes or until the brie is softened (15-20 minutes if using puff pastry).
6. Serve warm with crackers or sliced baguette.

2. Prosciutto-Wrapped Asparagus *Ingredients*:

- 1 lb (450 g) fresh asparagus, trimmed
- 12 slices of prosciutto
- Olive oil
- Freshly cracked black pepper

Instructions:

1. Preheat the oven to 400°F (200°C).
2. Wrap a slice of prosciutto around each asparagus spear, starting from the base and spiraling up to the tip.
3. Place on a baking sheet, drizzle with olive oil, and sprinkle with black pepper.
4. Bake for 10-15 minutes or until the asparagus is tender and the prosciutto is crispy.
5. Serve as an elegant appetizer or side dish.

The Main Course: The Heart of Christmas Dinner
3. Herb-Crusted Prime Rib with Horseradish Cream *Ingredi-ents*:

- 1 (5-6 lb) bone-in prime rib roast
- 3 tbsp olive oil
- 2 tbsp kosher salt
- 2 tbsp black pepper
- 1 tbsp garlic powder
- 2 tbsp fresh rosemary, chopped
- 2 tbsp fresh thyme, chopped
- 1 cup sour cream
- 2 tbsp prepared horseradish
- 1 tbsp lemon juice
- Salt and pepper to taste

Instructions:

1. Preheat the oven to 450°F (232°C). Let the roast come to room temperature for about an hour.
2. Mix olive oil, kosher salt, black pepper, garlic powder, rosemary, and thyme in a small bowl. Rub this mixture all over the roast.
3. Place the roast in a roasting pan with a rack and roast for 20 minutes.
4. Lower the oven temperature to 325°F (163°C) and continue roasting for 1.5-2 hours, or until a meat thermometer inserted into the center reads 130°F (54°C) for medium-rare.
5. Let the roast rest for 20 minutes before slicing.

6. For the horseradish cream, combine sour cream, horseradish, lemon juice, salt, and pepper in a bowl. Serve alongside the prime rib.

4. Stuffed Pork Loin with Apple and Sage *Ingredients*:

- 1 (3 lb) boneless pork loin
- 2 apples, peeled, cored, and diced
- 1/2 cup dried cranberries
- 1/2 cup breadcrumbs
- 2 tbsp fresh sage, chopped
- 1 tbsp butter
- Salt and pepper to taste

Instructions:

1. Preheat the oven to 375°F (190°C).
2. In a skillet, melt the butter and sauté the apples, cranberries, breadcrumbs, and sage until the apples are softened. Season with salt and pepper.
3. Butterfly the pork loin by slicing it lengthwise without cutting all the way through. Open it flat and spoon the apple mixture over the pork.
4. Roll up the pork loin and tie it with kitchen twine. Season the outside with salt and pepper.
5. Place in a roasting pan and bake for 1.5 hours or until the internal temperature reaches 145°F (63°C).
6. Let rest for 10 minutes before slicing.

Side Dishes: Complementing the Main Course
5. Honey-Glazed Carrots with Orange Zest *Ingredients*:

- 2 lbs (900 g) baby carrots
- 3 tbsp honey
- 2 tbsp butter
- Zest of 1 orange
- Salt and pepper to taste
- Fresh parsley for garnish

Instructions:

1. Boil the carrots in salted water for 5-7 minutes until tender. Drain and set aside.
2. In a large skillet, melt the butter and add the honey. Stir until combined.
3. Add the carrots to the skillet and toss until glazed. Season with salt, pepper, and orange zest.
4. Garnish with fresh parsley before serving.

6. Garlic and Herb Hasselback Potatoes *Ingredients*:

- 6 medium-sized potatoes
- 3 tbsp olive oil
- 4 cloves garlic, minced
- 2 tbsp fresh thyme, chopped
- 2 tbsp fresh rosemary, chopped
- Salt and pepper to taste

Instructions:

1. Preheat the oven to 425°F (218°C).
2. Slice the potatoes thinly, leaving the base intact to create a fan effect.
3. Mix olive oil, garlic, thyme, rosemary, salt, and pepper. Brush the mixture between the slices and over the tops of the potatoes.
4. Place the potatoes on a baking sheet and bake for 40-50 minutes or until crispy on the outside and tender on the inside.
5. Serve hot, garnished with additional herbs if desired.

Desserts: A Sweet Finish

7. Spiced Gingerbread Cake with Cream Cheese Frosting *Ingredients*:

- 2 1/2 cups all-purpose flour
- 2 tsp ground ginger
- 1 tsp ground cinnamon
- 1/2 tsp ground cloves
- 1/2 tsp salt
- 1/2 cup unsalted butter, softened
- 1 cup brown sugar
- 1 cup molasses
- 1 cup hot water
- 1 tsp baking soda
- 2 eggs

For the Frosting:

- 8 oz (225 g) cream cheese, softened
- 4 tbsp unsalted butter, softened
- 2 cups powdered sugar
- 1 tsp vanilla extract

Instructions:

1. Preheat the oven to 350°F (177°C). Grease a 9-inch square baking pan.
2. In a bowl, whisk flour, ginger, cinnamon, cloves, and salt.
3. In a large bowl, cream butter and brown sugar. Add the molasses and eggs, mixing well.
4. Dissolve baking soda in hot water and add to the wet mixture. Gradually add the dry ingredients.

5. Pour into the prepared pan and bake for 35-40 minutes or until a toothpick comes out clean.
6. For the frosting, beat the cream cheese and butter until fluffy. Add powdered sugar and vanilla, beating until smooth.
7. Once the cake has cooled, spread the frosting on top and garnish with a sprinkle of cinnamon or festive sprinkles.

8. Peppermint Chocolate Mousse *Ingredients*:

- 1 cup dark chocolate chips
- 2 tbsp sugar
- 1 cup heavy cream
- 1/2 tsp peppermint extract
- Crushed peppermint candies for garnish

Instructions:

1. Melt the chocolate chips in a double boiler or microwave, stirring until smooth.
2. In a bowl, beat the heavy cream and sugar until soft peaks form. Add peppermint extract and continue to beat until stiff peaks form.
3. Fold the melted chocolate into the whipped cream until well combined.
4. Spoon the mousse into serving glasses and refrigerate for 2 hours.
5. Garnish with crushed peppermint candies before serving.

Final Thoughts: Crafting a Memorable Feast

Christmas dinner is about more than just delicious food—it's a time to gather, reflect, and savor the moments spent with loved ones. By blending traditional recipes with new, creative twists, you create a meal that delights the senses and celebrates the season's spirit. Whether you're serving up classic prime rib or spiced gingerbread cake, these dishes will make your Christmas feast one that is cherished and remembered for years to come.

Chapter 8: Delectable Desserts and Drinks for the Holidays Original Recipes for Christmas Treats, Desserts, and Signature Holiday Drinks That Are Sure to Impress Guests

The holidays are a time for indulgence, and nothing completes a Christmas gathering like a spread of delectable desserts and festive drinks. These treats are more than just sweet finales to a meal—they're the centerpieces of parties, the focus of late-night gatherings, and the little joys that warm cold winter evenings. This chapter offers a collection of original recipes for holiday desserts and signature drinks that blend classic flavors with innovative twists to impress your guests and add an extra layer of magic to your celebrations.

Show-Stopping Holiday Desserts
1. White Chocolate Peppermint Cheesecake *Ingredients*:

- 2 cups crushed graham crackers
- 1/2 cup unsalted butter, melted
- 3 (8 oz) packages cream cheese, softened
- 1 cup sugar
- 3 large eggs
- 1 cup white chocolate, melted
- 1/2 cup sour cream
- 1/2 tsp peppermint extract
- Crushed peppermint candies for garnish
- Whipped cream for topping

Instructions:

1. Preheat the oven to 325°F (163°C). Grease a 9-inch springform pan.
2. Combine the crushed graham crackers and melted butter in a bowl. Press the mixture into the bottom of the prepared pan to form the crust.
3. In a large bowl, beat the cream cheese and sugar until smooth. Add the eggs one at a time, beating well after each addition.
4. Stir in the melted white chocolate, sour cream, and peppermint extract until fully combined.
5. Pour the filling over the crust and smooth the top. Bake for 50-60 minutes or until the center is set.
6. Let cool for 1 hour, then refrigerate for at least 4 hours.
7. Top with whipped cream and garnish with crushed peppermint candies before serving.

2. Cranberry Orange Bundt Cake with Vanilla Glaze *Ingredients*:

- 2 1/2 cups all-purpose flour
- 2 tsp baking powder
- 1/2 tsp baking soda
- 1/2 tsp salt
- 1 cup unsalted butter, softened
- 1 1/2 cups sugar
- 4 large eggs
- Zest of 1 orange
- 1/2 cup fresh orange juice
- 1/2 cup sour cream
- 1 1/2 cups fresh or frozen cranberries
- 1 cup powdered sugar (for glaze)
- 2-3 tbsp milk (for glaze)
- 1 tsp vanilla extract (for glaze)

Instructions:

1. Preheat the oven to 350°F (177°C). Grease a bundt pan thoroughly and dust with flour.
2. In a bowl, whisk together the flour, baking powder, baking soda, and salt.
3. In a large bowl, cream the butter and sugar until light and fluffy. Add the eggs one at a time, beating well after each.
4. Mix in the orange zest and orange juice.
5. Add the flour mixture in three parts, alternating with the sour cream, starting and ending with the flour mixture. Fold in the cranberries.
6. Pour the batter into the prepared bundt pan and smooth the top. Bake for 50-60 minutes or until a toothpick inserted comes out clean.

7. Let cool for 20 minutes in the pan before transferring to a wire rack.
8. For the glaze, whisk powdered sugar, milk, and vanilla extract. Drizzle over the cooled cake.

3. Spiced Eggnog Bread Pudding *Ingredients*:

- 6 cups cubed day-old brioche or challah bread
- 3 cups eggnog
- 4 large eggs
- 1/2 cup sugar
- 1 tsp cinnamon
- 1/2 tsp nutmeg
- 1 tsp vanilla extract
- 1/4 cup dark rum (optional)
- Whipped cream or vanilla ice cream for serving

Instructions:

1. Preheat the oven to 350°F (177°C). Grease a 9x13-inch baking dish.
2. Place the cubed bread in the baking dish.
3. In a large bowl, whisk together eggnog, eggs, sugar, cinnamon, nutmeg, vanilla extract, and rum.
4. Pour the eggnog mixture over the bread cubes and press down gently to ensure the bread absorbs the liquid.
5. Let sit for 10-15 minutes, then bake for 40-45 minutes or until golden brown and set.
6. Serve warm with whipped cream or vanilla ice cream.

4. Chocolate Hazelnut Yule Log *Ingredients*:

- 3/4 cup all-purpose flour
- 1/4 cup cocoa powder
- 1 tsp baking powder
- 1/2 tsp salt
- 4 large eggs, separated
- 3/4 cup sugar
- 1/2 tsp vanilla extract
- 1/2 cup Nutella or chocolate hazelnut spread
- 1 cup heavy cream, whipped
- Powdered sugar for dusting
- Chocolate shavings and fresh berries for garnish

Instructions:

1. Preheat the oven to 350°F (177°C). Line a 10x15-inch jelly roll pan with parchment paper.
2. In a bowl, sift together flour, cocoa powder, baking powder, and salt.
3. In another bowl, beat egg yolks and 1/2 cup sugar until thick and pale. Add vanilla extract.
4. In a separate bowl, beat egg whites until soft peaks form. Gradually add the remaining 1/4 cup sugar and continue beating until stiff peaks form.
5. Gently fold the dry ingredients into the egg yolk mixture, then fold in the egg whites in two parts.
6. Spread the batter evenly in the prepared pan and bake for 10-12 minutes.

7. Turn the cake out onto a clean, powdered sugar-dusted kitchen towel. Peel off the parchment paper and roll the cake up with the towel from the short side. Let cool completely.
8. Unroll and spread Nutella or chocolate hazelnut spread, followed by whipped cream. Reroll the cake (without the towel).
9. Dust with powdered sugar and decorate with chocolate shavings and berries.

Signature Holiday Drinks to Pair with Your Desserts
5. Spiced Mulled Wine *Ingredients*:

- 1 bottle of red wine (Merlot or Cabernet Sauvignon)
- 1/4 cup brandy
- 1/2 cup orange juice
- 1/4 cup honey or sugar
- 2 cinnamon sticks
- 4 whole cloves
- 3 star anise
- 1 orange, sliced
- 1 apple, sliced

Instructions:

1. Combine wine, brandy, orange juice, and honey in a large pot.
2. Add cinnamon sticks, cloves, star anise, orange slices, and apple slices.
3. Heat over low heat until just below simmering (do not boil) for 20-25 minutes.
4. Strain and serve warm in heatproof glasses. Garnish with a cinnamon stick or orange slice.

6. Peppermint White Hot Chocolate *Ingredients*:

- 4 cups whole milk
- 1 cup white chocolate chips
- 1/2 tsp peppermint extract
- Whipped cream for topping
- Crushed peppermint candies for garnish

Instructions:

1. In a saucepan, heat the milk over medium heat until hot (do not boil).
2. Add white chocolate chips and whisk until melted and smooth.
3. Stir in peppermint extract and remove from heat.
4. Pour into mugs and top with whipped cream and crushed peppermint candies.

7. Gingerbread Eggnog Martini *Ingredients*:

- 2 oz eggnog
- 1 oz vodka
- 1 oz coffee liqueur
- 1/2 tsp ground ginger
- Ice
- Whipped cream for garnish
- Gingerbread cookie or cinnamon stick for garnish

Instructions:

1. Fill a shaker with ice and add eggnog, vodka, coffee liqueur, and ground ginger.
2. Shake well and strain into a chilled martini glass.

3. Top with whipped cream and garnish with a gingerbread cookie or cinnamon stick.

8. Holiday Cranberry Spritzer *Ingredients*:

- 2 cups cranberry juice
- 1 cup sparkling water or club soda
- 1/4 cup orange juice
- 1/4 cup pomegranate seeds
- Orange slices for garnish
- Fresh mint leaves for garnish

Instructions:

1. In a large pitcher, combine cranberry juice and orange juice.
2. Add sparkling water and stir gently.
3. Pour into glasses and top with pomegranate seeds, orange slices, and mint leaves.
4. Serve chilled or over ice for a refreshing holiday drink.

Final Thoughts: The Sweetest Part of the Season

Christmas desserts and drinks are the crowning touch to your holiday gatherings, offering opportunities to showcase creativity and indulgence. These recipes blend traditional flavors with modern twists to create a spread that's sure to delight every palate. From a show-stopping peppermint cheesecake to the comforting embrace of a spiced mulled wine, these recipes bring the joy and festivity of the season to your table. Let this be the year where your holiday sweets and drinks become the talk of the season, adding warmth and sweetness to every celebration.

Chapter 9: Gift-Wrapping as an Art Form

Creative and Sustainable Gift-Wrapping Ideas, Including DIY Wrapping Paper, Reusable Materials, and Nature-Inspired Touches

Gift-wrapping is more than just covering a present; it's a way to show thoughtfulness, enhance anticipation, and add a personal touch to your gifts. In an era where sustainability is key, finding ways to wrap presents that are both beautiful and environmentally friendly has become an art in itself. This chapter explores creative and sustainable gift-wrapping ideas, from DIY wrapping paper to reusable materials and nature-inspired touches that will make your presents stand out under the tree.

The Art and Significance of Gift-Wrapping

Gift-wrapping has long been a symbol of love and care. The time spent choosing the perfect wrapping and adorning a gift with special details adds a layer of thoughtfulness that enhances the joy of giving. This chapter encourages a shift from conventional, often wasteful wrapping practices to more sustainable, creative methods that reflect a commitment to both beauty and environmental responsibility.

Sustainable and Eco-Friendly Gift-Wrapping Materials

1. DIY Wrapping Paper Creating your own wrapping paper adds a personal touch and allows you to recycle and repurpose materials you may already have at home.

- *Brown Kraft Paper*: A versatile and biodegradable option that can be decorated in countless ways. Use stamps, hand-drawn designs, or stencils to customize it.
- *Potato Stamp Art*: Carve simple shapes like stars, trees, or snowflakes into halved potatoes and use non-toxic paint to create unique, repeatable patterns on kraft paper.

- *Newspaper and Sheet Music*: Repurpose old newspapers, book pages, or sheet music for a vintage, artistic look. Add a splash of color with a red or green ribbon or twine for contrast.

2. Reusable Fabrics and Wraps Opting for reusable wraps not only reduces waste but also adds a sophisticated touch to your gifts.

- *Furoshiki (Japanese Fabric Wrapping)*: A traditional method of wrapping gifts in fabric. Use square pieces of fabric, scarves, or cloth napkins in festive colors or patterns. These wraps can be tied in various ways to create beautiful folds and knots.
- *Tea Towels or Kitchen Cloths*: For gifts going to food lovers or homemakers, wrap presents in decorative tea towels or kitchen cloths that can be reused.
- *Fabric Gift Bags*: Sew or purchase reusable cloth gift bags in different sizes. Add a drawstring or ribbon for a polished look.

3. Upcycled and Recycled Materials Embrace creative reuse with these eco-friendly materials:

- *Maps and Calendars*: Old maps and wall calendars with vibrant imagery make for unique and eye-catching gift wrap.
- *Paper Bags*: Decorate plain paper grocery bags with stamps, drawings, or cut-out designs for a rustic, personal touch.
- *Leftover Wallpaper*: Pieces of wallpaper offer a durable and patterned alternative to traditional wrapping paper.

Nature-Inspired Gift-Wrapping Touches

1. Greenery and Natural Adornments Incorporating natural elements into your wrapping gives it an elegant, earthy feel.

- *Evergreen Sprigs*: Use small branches of pine, cedar, or rosemary as decorative accents. Tuck them under the ribbon or tie them onto the bow for a fragrant, festive touch.
- *Cinnamon Sticks and Dried Oranges*: Attach a few cinnamon sticks or a slice of dried orange to the ribbon for an aromatic and visually appealing addition.
- *Pinecones and Acorns*: Small pinecones or acorns can be hot-glued to gift tags or used as standalone decorations. Spray-paint them gold or silver for a touch of glam.

2. Twine and Burlap Replace plastic ribbons with natural fibers like jute twine or burlap strips.

- *Jute Twine*: Wrap gifts with jute twine for a rustic look. Pair it with brown paper and a sprig of greenery for a minimalist, nature-inspired effect.
- *Burlap Ribbons*: Use burlap as a ribbon or band around the center of your gift. Combine it with lace for an elegant touch that contrasts beautifully with the rough texture.

Personalizing Your Gift-Wrapping

1. Handcrafted Gift Tags Create unique gift tags using sustainable materials.

- *Recycled Cardboard*: Cut out gift tags from cardboard boxes or cereal packages. Use stamps, calligraphy, or hand-drawn designs to personalize them.
- *Pressed Leaves and Flowers*: Glue pressed leaves or small dried flowers onto blank tags for a delicate, nature-inspired look.
- *Photos as Tags*: Print small photos of the recipient and use them as gift tags. This adds a special, personal touch and becomes a keepsake.

2. Custom Decorative Touches Make each gift one-of-a-kind with small decorative additions.

- *Buttons and Beads*: Sew or glue buttons and beads onto ribbons or paper for a playful, decorative touch.
- *Mini Ornaments*: Tie small ornaments, such as stars or bells, onto the ribbon. This adds a festive detail that can be reused as tree ornaments.
- *Handwritten Notes*: Instead of store-bought cards, write a personal note or poem on the gift wrap itself. Use a metallic or white pen for contrast on darker papers.

Innovative Wrapping Techniques

1. Layered Wraps Create depth and texture by layering different types of wrapping materials.

- *Double Wrap*: Wrap the gift in plain brown paper first, then layer a strip of patterned or fabric wrap around the center.
- *Cut-Out Overlays*: Use an X-Acto knife to create simple cut-out designs in a layer of wrapping paper and place it over a different color or patterned sheet. The underlying pattern will show through the cut-outs for a striking effect.

2. The "Envelope" Wrap For smaller gifts, try an envelope-style wrap.

- *Triangular Fold*: Place the gift at one corner of the paper and fold over each side to create an envelope shape. Secure it with twine or a decorative seal.
- *Button Closure*: Add buttons and twine to create a flap closure that can be opened and reused.

3. Basket Wrapping For a unique and reusable alternative, place gifts in small baskets or decorative boxes.

- *Miniature Gift Baskets*: Line the basket with tissue paper or fabric and arrange gifts inside. Top it off with a ribbon or bow.
- *Decorative Wooden Crates*: Use small wooden crates for larger items and embellish them with holiday ribbons and natural elements like pinecones and sprigs.

Tips for Wrapping Unconventionally Shaped Gifts

1. Use Fabric Wrap irregularly shaped items in large pieces of fabric or scarves that can easily mold to the shape of the object.

2. Create Custom Boxes Repurpose cardboard to create boxes or containers tailored to fit unusual shapes. Decorate them with paint or recycled paper.

3. Drawstring Bags Sew or purchase drawstring bags that can fit snugly around items like plush toys, plants, or bottles. These bags are both convenient and reusable.

Final Thoughts: Wrapping with Thoughtfulness and Care

Wrapping gifts is more than a task; it's an opportunity to express creativity, care, and consideration for the environment. By incorporating DIY techniques, reusable materials, and nature-inspired details, you can turn gift-wrapping into an art form that enhances the joy of giving. Let your gift-wrapping be a reflection of your holiday spirit and thoughtfulness, creating an experience as memorable as the gift itself.

Chapter 10: Secret Santa and Creative Gift Exchanges

Fun Twists on Secret Santa, White Elephant Exchanges, and Other Group Gift-Giving Games to Make Them Memorable and Engaging

Gift exchanges are one of the most enjoyable aspects of the holiday season, bringing groups together through the excitement of giving and receiving. While traditional Secret Santa and White Elephant gift exchanges are beloved staples, adding unique twists can make these games even more engaging and memorable. This chapter provides extensive ideas and detailed guidance for spicing up your holiday gift-giving games, ensuring that everyone involved has a great time and leaves with a story to tell.

The Classic Secret Santa and How to Enhance It

What is Secret Santa? Secret Santa is a gift exchange game where participants draw names to determine who they will buy a gift for, with the identity of the gift-giver remaining a secret until the gift is revealed. While this format is timeless, adding fun variations can elevate the experience.

1. Themed Secret Santa

- *Color Theme*: Set a rule where all gifts must be based on a specific color, such as "red-themed" gifts for the holiday season. This adds a creative challenge for participants and results in beautifully co-ordinated gifts.

- *Hobbies Theme*: Have participants fill out a brief questionnaire listing their hobbies or interests, and draw names accordingly. This ensures that gifts are more personalized and thoughtful.

- *Budget Challenge*: Choose an unusual or tight budget (e.g., under $5 or exactly $10) to encourage creativity and ingenuity in gift selection.

2. Secret Santa with Clues Turn the traditional format into a guessing game by adding clues:

- *Clue Cards*: Each participant includes a written clue about their identity with their gift. Before opening gifts, the group can take turns guessing who their Secret Santa might be based on the clues provided.
- *Scavenger Hunt*: Instead of handing the gift directly, have participants hide their gifts around the venue and leave clues leading to the location. This adds an element of fun and anticipation.

3. Secret Santa Storytime

- *Personalized Stories*: When the recipient opens their gift, the giver tells a short story or shares a memory related to the item (without revealing themselves right away). This creates a warm, storytelling atmosphere and makes the exchange more heartfelt.
- *Riddles and Poems*: The Secret Santa writes a riddle or poem hinting at their identity or the gift itself. Recipients must solve it before opening the present.

White Elephant with a Twist

What is White Elephant? White Elephant (also known as Yankee Swap) is a game where participants bring wrapped gifts and take turns choosing a gift or stealing an already chosen gift from another player. It's often played with humorous or inexpensive gifts, leading to surprises and laughs.

1. Themed White Elephant

- *Gag Gifts Only*: Make the rule that all gifts must be humorous or "useless" items. This version is great for lighthearted gatherings where laughter is the main goal.
- *Cozy Gifts*: Set a theme where all gifts must be related to comfort, such as blankets, slippers, or hot cocoa sets. This ensures that everyone goes home with something they can enjoy during the colder months.
- *Vintage Finds*: Require that all gifts be second-hand or antique items. This twist encourages participants to visit thrift stores or antique shops, leading to unique and interesting gifts.

2. The "Steal or Reveal" Variation Add a new layer of choice by allowing participants to either steal a gift from someone or reveal their chosen gift to everyone before they make a final decision. If they reveal it, they must keep it, and if they choose to steal, the round continues as usual.

3. Mystery Box Edition Introduce a "mystery box" into the mix. The box could contain anything, from a fantastic prize to a quirky, funny item. Participants can choose to pick from the standard gifts or risk choosing the mystery box. The catch? Once chosen, the box can't be stolen, adding suspense to the game.

4. Dice Game White Elephant Assign dice rolls to specific actions:

- Roll a 1: Swap your gift with anyone.
- Roll a 2: Open your gift.
- Roll a 3: Pick a new gift.
- Roll a 4: Steal a gift that's been opened.
- Roll a 5: Everyone passes their gift to the right.
- Roll a 6: Choose someone to open their gift. This variation adds an unpredictable element and keeps everyone on their toes.

Creative Gift Exchange Games for Groups
1. Musical Gifts

- *How It Works*: Similar to musical chairs, participants sit in a circle and pass gifts around while music plays. When the music stops, the gift each person is holding becomes theirs to keep. For an added twist, gifts could be unwrapped as they are passed, building anticipation.
- *Variation*: The gift-passing can include small rules, such as changing direction or requiring a participant to switch their gift with another person when the music stops.

2. The "Guess the Giver" Game

- *How It Works*: Each participant brings a gift with no tag indicating who it's from. After all gifts are distributed and opened, everyone takes turns guessing who brought which gift. Each correct guess earns points, and the person with the most points wins a small prize.
- *Bonus Challenge*: Givers must bring gifts that subtly reflect their personality or interests, making the guessing more challenging and personal.

3. Gift Auction

- *How It Works*: Give each participant a set number of "bidding tokens" (like paper money or chips). Each gift is placed on a table, wrapped, and auctioned off one by one. Participants must bid for the gifts they want, adding strategic fun and competitive excitement to the exchange.
- *Variation*: Include a "blind bid" option where gifts are auctioned without anyone knowing what's inside. This adds an element of surprise to the bidding process.

4. The Left-Right Gift Game

- *How It Works*: Each participant starts with a gift in hand. A story is read aloud, and each time the words "left" or "right" are said, everyone passes their gift in that direction. When the story ends, each person keeps the gift they're holding.
- *Crafting the Story*: Personalize the story to include inside jokes or holiday themes to make it more enjoyable and engaging.

5. Holiday Grab Bag

- *How It Works*: Participants place all gifts in a bag or a large container. Each person takes turns reaching in (without looking) and grabbing a gift. They can choose to keep the gift or pass it to the next person, adding an element of chance and surprise.
- *Timed Variation*: Add a timer, giving each participant only a few seconds to decide if they want to keep or pass the gift.

6. Re-Gift Game

- *How It Works*: Everyone brings a "re-gifted" item from their home—something useful but not new. This game can lead to interesting stories about why the item was originally received and who it's best suited for.
- *Rules*: Limit gifts to clean, functional items, avoiding gag gifts or broken items.

Tips for Making Gift Exchanges More Fun and Inclusive
1. Set Clear Guidelines

- Ensure everyone knows the rules and budget in advance to avoid confusion.
- For themed exchanges, clearly communicate the theme and expectations so that participants have enough time to prepare.

2. Keep Gifts Balanced

- Encourage everyone to bring gifts of similar value to maintain fairness and excitement.
- Suggest fun, universal items like board games, books, gourmet snacks, or cozy blankets if people are unsure what to bring.

3. Add Prizes for Winners

- Introduce small prizes for participants who win certain aspects of the game, such as "Best Guesser" in the "Guess the Giver" game or the "Highest Bidder" in the Gift Auction.

4. Incorporate Food and Drinks

- Pair gift exchanges with festive drinks and snacks. A hot cocoa bar, mulled wine, or a tray of Christmas cookies will make the experience more enjoyable and relaxed.

5. Create a Festive Atmosphere

- Play holiday music in the background to set the mood and keep everyone energized.
- Decorate the space with holiday lights, garlands, and a festive table centerpiece to enhance the ambiance.

Final Thoughts: Making Gift Exchanges Unforgettable

Whether it's a classic Secret Santa with a twist, a chaotic White Elephant game, or a creative new gift-giving game, adding unique variations can make your holiday gathering more fun and memorable. The key to a successful gift exchange is ensuring that everyone feels included and has a good time. Choose an idea that fits your group's sense of humor, style, and interests, and let the holiday spirit infuse each moment with laughter, surprise, and joy.

Chapter 11: Mindful Gifting – Choosing Meaningful Presents

Guidance on Choosing Gifts That Truly Resonate, Including Handmade, Eco-Friendly, and Experiential Gifts

In the hustle and bustle of holiday shopping, it's easy to fall into the trap of buying gifts out of obligation rather than intention. However, mindful gifting—choosing presents that truly resonate with the recipient—creates deeper connections and memories. Thoughtful gifts reflect consideration, shared experiences, and values, making them treasured long after the holiday season ends. This chapter provides detailed guidance on selecting meaningful presents, exploring handmade, eco-friendly, and experiential gifts that will touch hearts and leave lasting impressions.

The Art of Mindful Gifting

Mindful gifting begins with understanding the recipient's personality, interests, and needs. Instead of focusing on the latest trends or expensive items, consider what would bring true joy and value. Ask yourself questions like:

- What are their hobbies or interests?
- What would support their well-being or growth?
- What experiences or memories can you share with them?

By answering these questions, you can approach gift-giving with thoughtfulness and purpose, ensuring your gifts foster joy, connection, and sustainability.

Handmade Gifts: Adding a Personal Touch

Handmade gifts convey love and effort, making them cherished tokens that recipients appreciate. Crafting your own presents allows you to personalize gifts in unique ways that commercial items cannot replicate.

1. Customized Gift Baskets

- *How to Create*: Choose a theme that suits the recipient's interests, such as a "self-care basket" with handmade bath bombs, essential oils, and candles, or a "baker's kit" with specialty flours, recipe cards, and a custom apron.
- *Personal Touch*: Add handwritten notes or labels explaining the significance of each item, making the gift feel even more special.

2. Homemade Edibles

- *Jars of Goodness*: Layer the dry ingredients for cookies, brownies, or hot cocoa mix in a decorative jar. Attach a handwritten recipe card for easy instructions.
- *Infused Oils or Flavored Salts*: Create homemade rosemary-infused olive oil, chili oil, or flavored salts (e.g., lemon-thyme salt). Package them in glass bottles or jars tied with twine for a rustic look.
- *Baked Goods*: Personalize baked treats like shortbread cookies, homemade granola, or artisan bread, and package them in sustainable containers like reusable tins or cloth wraps.

3. DIY Crafts and Personalized Art

- *Hand-Painted Mugs*: Customize plain ceramic mugs with paint pens or ceramic-safe paint. Decorate them with the recipient's favorite quotes, animals, or patterns.

- *Knitted or Crocheted Gifts*: Scarves, hats, and blankets are practical and cozy gifts that show dedication and care.
- *Photo Collage or Scrapbook*: Compile memories in a personalized scrapbook or frame a photo collage that celebrates shared experiences.

Eco-Friendly Gifts: Giving Thoughtfully for a Sustainable Future

Choosing eco-friendly gifts demonstrates a commitment to mindful living and helps reduce environmental impact. Sustainable presents are often well-crafted, ethical, and long-lasting.

1. Sustainable Lifestyle Products

- *Reusable Kitchenware*: Gift items like stainless steel water bottles, bamboo cutlery sets, beeswax food wraps, or reusable coffee cups.
- *Eco-Friendly Beauty Kits*: Put together a kit with biodegradable makeup remover pads, solid shampoos, handmade soaps, and organic lotions.
- *Natural Fiber Clothing*: Look for items made from organic cotton, bamboo, or sustainable fabrics that align with the recipient's style and preferences.

2. Plants and Green Gifts

- *Potted Houseplants*: Indoor plants like pothos, snake plants, or succulents make wonderful gifts that purify the air and brighten a space.
- *Herb Gardens*: Create a small indoor herb garden kit with pots, soil, and seeds for herbs like basil, thyme, and rosemary.
- *Seed Bombs*: Handmade seed bombs made from native wildflower seeds wrapped in eco-friendly packaging can be a fun gift for gardening enthusiasts.

3. Gifts that Reduce Waste

- *Zero-Waste Starter Kits*: Assemble kits with items like reusable straws, mesh produce bags, cloth napkins, and bamboo toothbrushes.
- *Upcycled Gifts*: Find or create items made from repurposed materials, such as recycled glass vases, upcycled denim bags, or furniture refurbished with eco-friendly paints.

Experiential Gifts: Creating Memories That Last

Experiential gifts go beyond material items, offering the gift of time, adventure, and cherished memories. These gifts are perfect for those who value quality experiences and connections.

1. Event Tickets and Passes

- *Concerts and Shows*: Purchase tickets to a concert, theater production, or comedy show featuring the recipient's favorite performers.
- *Sports Events*: For sports enthusiasts, consider tickets to a game or match they'd love to attend.
- *Cultural Passes*: Gift memberships or passes to local museums, art galleries, or botanical gardens for an enriching experience.

2. Workshops and Classes

- *Cooking Classes*: Arrange for a cooking class that aligns with their culinary interests, such as baking, sushi-making, or pasta workshops.
- *Art and Craft Sessions*: Sign them up for pottery, painting, or photography classes that can help them develop new skills.
- *Fitness and Wellness*: Gift yoga classes, a wellness retreat, or a personal training session for those interested in health and mindfulness.

3. Getaways and Travel Experiences

- *Weekend Getaway*: Plan a weekend trip to a cozy cabin, beachside resort, or mountain lodge for a much-needed break.
- *Adventure Experiences*: For thrill-seekers, book activities like zip-lining, hot air balloon rides, or guided hikes.
- *Staycation Package*: Create a "staycation" gift that includes local dining vouchers, movie passes, and spa treatments for a relaxing time close to home.

4. Subscription Services

- *Meal Kit Deliveries*: For the busy cook, a meal kit subscription can be a practical and exciting way to try new recipes.
- *Book Club Subscriptions*: Monthly book deliveries tailored to their genre of choice make perfect gifts for avid readers.
- *Streaming Services*: A gift subscription to a movie, TV, or music streaming service can provide hours of entertainment.

Personalized and Thoughtful Gifting Ideas
1. Customized Gifts

- *Monogrammed Items*: Personalize gifts like towels, robes, or note-books with their initials.
- *Custom Jewelry*: Choose jewelry with their birthstone or engrave a meaningful date or name.
- *Artisan-Made Goods*: Support local or small businesses by gifting hand-crafted items that reflect the recipient's style, such as pottery, woven baskets, or handmade candles.

2. Sentimental Gifts

- *Memory Jar*: Fill a jar with handwritten notes recounting fond memories, inside jokes, or reasons why you appreciate the person.
- *Time Capsule*: Create a "holiday time capsule" with small, meaningful items and notes that can be opened in a year.
- *Personalized Calendar*: Use photos of shared moments to create a custom calendar, with each month featuring a special memory.

3. Gifts That Give Back

- *Charitable Donations*: Make a donation in the recipient's name to a charity or cause that is meaningful to them.
- *Fair-Trade Gifts*: Choose gifts from organizations that prioritize ethical production practices, supporting artisans and communities worldwide.
- *Eco-Conscious Brands*: Opt for brands that are committed to sustainability, using recycled materials and green manufacturing processes.

Tips for Mindful Gifting

1. Consider the Recipient's Values Think about what is important to the person receiving the gift. Avid environmentalists will appreciate sustainable and upcycled items, while experience-seekers may prefer a memorable activity over a physical gift.

2. Quality Over Quantity Focus on one meaningful, high-quality gift rather than several less thoughtful items. This approach reinforces the idea that it's the thought and intention behind the gift that matters most.

3. Presentation Matters Even when choosing eco-friendly or handmade gifts, how you present them counts. Use sustainable wrapping methods, such as reusable fabric, recycled paper, or biodegradable twine, to complete the experience.

4. Add a Personal Note A handwritten note or card expressing your thoughts adds a heartfelt touch to any gift. It shows that you've taken the time to consider why the gift is special and what the recipient means to you.

Final Thoughts: The Heart of Gifting

Mindful gifting is about creating connections and showing that you care. Whether through a handmade creation, an eco-friendly product, or an unforgettable experience, choosing gifts that resonate with the recipient can make the holiday season more meaningful for both the giver and the receiver. Let your gifts be an expression of love, thoughtfulness, and shared values, ensuring that they are cherished long after the holidays have passed.

Chapter 12: Creating the Ultimate Christmas Photo Album
Tips on Capturing the Best Holiday Moments, Organizing Photos, and Creating a Memorable Digital or Physical Album

The holiday season is filled with cherished moments that deserve to be preserved for years to come. Creating a Christmas photo album is a beautiful way to document these memories and relive the joy of the season whenever you open its pages. Whether you prefer a digital album or a traditional physical one, this chapter will guide you through capturing the best holiday moments, organizing your photos, and designing an album that tells your holiday story in the most meaningful way possible.

Capturing the Best Holiday Moments

Photography during the holidays can be challenging, as festivities are filled with movement, varied lighting, and fleeting moments. However, with a few key strategies, you can ensure your Christmas photos capture the magic and warmth of the season.

1. Plan Ahead

- *Scout the Best Locations*: Identify key spots in your home or holiday venue with good natural light and festive decor. This could be in front of the Christmas tree, by the fireplace, or near a window adorned with garlands.
- *Create a Shot List*: Make a list of must-capture moments, such as opening presents, decorating the tree, Christmas dinner, family hugs, and candid laughter. This helps ensure that no special moment is overlooked.

2. Master Lighting

- *Use Natural Light*: Whenever possible, take photos near windows or during the daytime for a soft, natural glow. Golden hour (the hour after sunrise or before sunset) provides particularly warm, flattering light.
- *Embrace Low-Light Photography*: For evening shots, use ambient light from the Christmas tree, candles, or fairy lights to create a cozy atmosphere. Adjust your camera or smartphone settings to increase exposure and reduce motion blur.
- *Avoid Harsh Flash*: Direct flash can create unflattering shadows and wash out your subjects. Instead, use a diffuser or bounce the light off a ceiling or wall for softer illumination.

3. Candid Shots vs. Posed Photos

- *Capture Genuine Reactions*: Candid photos often tell the most compelling stories. Keep your camera or smartphone handy to capture spontaneous moments, such as a child's wide-eyed wonder when they see their gifts or friends sharing a laugh during dinner.
- *Take Group Portraits*: While candid shots are essential, posed group photos are also important for family keepsakes. Use a tripod and self-timer for larger groups or enlist someone to take the photo so everyone is included.

4. Composition and Angles

- *Use the Rule of Thirds*: Divide your frame into thirds, both vertically and horizontally, and place your subjects along these lines for a balanced and visually appealing composition.
- *Change Up the Angles*: Experiment with different perspectives. Take photos from above when decorating cookies or from ground level for a child's-eye view of opening presents. Capturing scenes from unique angles adds depth and interest.
- *Focus on Details*: Don't just photograph people—zoom in on holiday details like ornaments, table settings, wrapped gifts, and homemade treats. These small touches help tell a complete story.

5. Editing Tips for a Polished Look

- *Use Editing Apps*: Enhance your photos using simple editing apps like Lightroom, Snapseed, or built-in photo editors on smartphones. Adjust brightness, contrast, and color balance for a polished finish.
- *Keep Edits Natural*: Avoid over-editing with heavy filters or extreme color saturation. Aim for edits that enhance rather than alter the photo's natural beauty.
- *Black and White for Emphasis*: Convert a few select photos to black and white for a timeless, classic touch that emphasizes emotion and contrast.

Organizing Your Holiday Photos

After a holiday gathering, you may find yourself with hundreds of photos. Organizing them efficiently is crucial to creating an album that is both coherent and meaningful.

1. Sort and Select the Best Photos

- *Delete Duplicates*: Go through your collection and remove duplicate shots or photos with blurs and imperfections.
- *Choose a Mix*: Select a variety of photos, including group shots, candids, and detail images, to create a balanced album.
- *Highlight Key Moments*: Pick photos that represent the flow of the day, such as opening gifts, enjoying a meal, or decorating the tree.

2. Create Folders and Categories

- *Chronological Organization*: Arrange photos in the order they were taken to create a natural timeline of the day's events.
- *Thematic Grouping*: Group photos by theme (e.g., "Decorating the Tree," "Christmas Morning," "Dinner Table") for easy access and storytelling.
- *Use Labels or Tags*: Add labels or tags to photos based on people, locations, or events to help you find them quickly.

3. Backup and Storage

- *Cloud Storage*: Store your photos on a cloud service like Google Photos, Dropbox, or iCloud to ensure they're safe and accessible from any device.
- *External Hard Drive*: Keep a backup of your holiday photos on an external hard drive for added security and peace of mind.

Creating a Memorable Digital Photo Album

Digital photo albums are a convenient way to share holiday memories with friends and family and can be easily accessed from anywhere. Here's how to make a standout digital album:

1. Choose the Right Platform

- *Online Services*: Platforms like Shutterfly, Snapfish, or Blurb offer customizable templates and printing options for digital albums.
- *DIY Software*: Use design software such as Canva or Adobe InDesign for more creative freedom and personalized layouts.
- *Social Media Albums*: Create a private Facebook album or use Instagram Stories Highlights to share with family and friends.

2. Customize Your Layout

- *Choose a Theme*: Select a holiday or winter theme to tie your album together visually. Opt for festive backgrounds, colors, and fonts that match the season's aesthetic.
- *Mix Layouts*: Alternate between full-page photos, collages, and pages with text to keep the viewer engaged.
- *Add Text and Captions*: Write captions that describe the moments, include funny anecdotes, or quote conversations from the day.

3. Interactive Elements

- *Video Clips*: Incorporate short video clips or GIFs that capture action moments like gift-opening or dancing.
- *Background Music*: Some digital albums allow you to add background music for an immersive experience. Choose holiday classics or instrumental tracks for a warm touch.

Designing a Stunning Physical Photo Album

There's something special about flipping through a physical photo album and feeling the weight of memories in your hands. Creating a printed album requires careful thought but is well worth the effort.

1. Select a High-Quality Album

- *Hardcover Albums*: Opt for a sturdy hardcover album for a timeless, durable keepsake.
- *Layflat Binding*: Choose layflat pages for seamless, panoramic spreads that are perfect for showcasing group photos and double-page images.

2. Arrange Photos Creatively

- *Storytelling Flow*: Arrange photos to tell the story of your holiday from start to finish. Use larger photos for impactful moments and smaller ones for supporting details.
- *Mix Photos and Memorabilia*: Include items like holiday cards, tickets, or handwritten notes for added texture and personalization.
- *Design with White Space*: Leave enough white space between photos to avoid a cluttered look and allow each image to stand out.

3. Add Decorative Details

- *Scrapbook Elements*: Use stickers, washi tape, and stamps to add decorative touches. Holiday-themed embellishments can enhance the festive feel.
- *Handwritten Captions*: Write captions by hand for a personal touch. Use metallic or colored pens to make them stand out.

- *Photo Corners and Frames*: Use decorative photo corners or mini-frames to add dimension and keep your photos in place.

4. Personalize the Cover

- *Title and Date*: Add a title like "Christmas 2023" or "Our Holiday Memories" and include the year for easy reference.
- *Photo Collage Cover*: Choose a favorite photo or create a collage for the cover to make the album instantly recognizable.
- *Embossing and Foiling*: For an elegant touch, consider embossing or foiling the cover with gold or silver accents.

Tips for Keeping Your Album Engaging

1. Balance Photos and Text Add brief anecdotes, jokes, or reflections to accompany photos. This turns your album into a storybook that captures both images and the emotions behind them.

2. Vary Your Photo Sizes Mix full-page photos with smaller clusters to create visual interest. Reserve full pages for group shots or significant moments and use smaller spaces for detail shots.

3. Include Candid Shots While posed photos are lovely, candid shots often hold the most genuine expressions and interactions. These are the moments that capture the spirit of the day.

4. Print Quality Matters Select high-quality printing options with thick, matte, or glossy paper that enhances the colors and detail of your photos. This will make your album feel premium and last for years.

Final Thoughts: Crafting a Legacy of Memories

A well-curated Christmas photo album is more than just a collection of pictures—it's a keepsake filled with stories, love, and cherished moments that you and your loved ones can revisit time and time again. Whether you choose a digital format for easy sharing or a physical album to display on your coffee table, taking the time to organize and design your album thoughtfully will create a legacy of holiday memories that lasts a lifetime. Make this season unforgettable by capturing its magic in a format that reflects the joy and warmth of your Christmas celebrations.

Chapter 13: Christmas Around the World – Embracing Global Traditions

Insight into How Other Cultures Celebrate Christmas, Inspiring Readers to Integrate Global Traditions

Christmas is celebrated in many countries around the world, each infusing the holiday with its unique customs, flavors, and traditions. Exploring these diverse celebrations can enrich our understanding of the holiday and inspire new ways to enjoy the season with loved ones. By embracing global traditions, we can create a more inclusive and meaningful Christmas that reflects the shared joy of the season while appreciating cultural diversity. This chapter delves into how different cultures celebrate Christmas and offers tips on incorporating these traditions into your own holiday festivities.

The Beauty of Diverse Celebrations

Every culture brings its distinctive flair to Christmas, shaped by history, beliefs, and regional customs. Whether through food, music, decorations, or community rituals, these traditions illuminate the universal themes of love, generosity, and togetherness. By exploring these global practices, we can adopt elements that resonate with us and create a celebration that's uniquely our own.

European Christmas Traditions

1. Germany: The Birthplace of Many Holiday Customs Germany is known for its rich Christmas traditions, many of which have influenced how the holiday is celebrated worldwide.

- *Christmas Markets (Weihnachtsmärkte)*: These festive markets, brimming with lights, crafts, and food stalls, are held in town squares across Germany. They sell everything from handcrafted gifts to mulled wine (Glühwein). *Inspiration*: Host a small Christmas market at home or in your community, complete with stalls offering handmade crafts, cookies, and warm drinks.

- *Advent Calendar and Advent Wreath*: The advent calendar, often filled with small treats or toys, is a popular tradition. The Advent wreath, adorned with four candles, is lit one by one each Sunday leading up to Christmas. *Inspiration*: Create a homemade advent calendar or wreath using greenery, ribbons, and small trinkets for a fun, weekly ritual.

2. Italy: La Festa and Nativity Displays Christmas in Italy is steeped in religious and family traditions.

- *Feast of the Seven Fishes*: On Christmas Eve, Italian families often partake in a seafood feast, known as La Vigilia. This meal includes an array of fish dishes that symbolize abstinence from meat. *Inspiration*: Incorporate a seafood dish or host a themed dinner to honor this Italian tradition.
- *Nativity Scenes (Presepe)*: Italians are famous for their elaborate nativity displays, which often depict not just the Holy Family but entire village scenes with intricate details. *Inspiration*: Create your own nativity scene using handcrafted or unique figurines, adding elements that reflect your family's personality.

3. Sweden: The Feast of St. Lucia St. Lucia's Day, celebrated on December 13, is a major event in Sweden that marks the beginning of the Christmas season.

- *Procession of Light*: Girls dressed in white gowns with red sashes and wreaths of candles on their heads lead processions, singing carols to symbolize the triumph of light over darkness. *Inspiration*: Incorporate a small candlelight procession at home or teach children about the story of St. Lucia while enjoying Swedish treats like saffron buns (Lussekatter).

Latin American Christmas Celebrations
4. Mexico: Las Posadas and Festive Piñatas In Mexico, Christmas is a deeply spiritual and festive time filled with community-centered events.

- *Las Posadas*: This nine-day celebration reenacts Mary and Joseph's search for lodging in Bethlehem. Each evening, processions are held where participants sing, pray, and knock on doors until they find "shelter," leading to a fiesta. *Inspiration*: Host a mini Las Posadas celebration with friends or family, ending with a party that includes traditional Mexican food and music.
- *Piñatas*: During Posadas and Christmas parties, colorful piñatas filled with candy and toys are broken open by children. *Inspiration*: Integrate a piñata into your holiday festivities for a fun and playful touch that will delight kids and adults alike.

5. Brazil: Midnight Mass and Festive Feasts In Brazil, Christmas is marked by vibrant gatherings and a strong emphasis on religious observance.

- *Missa do Galo (Midnight Mass)*: Attending Midnight Mass on Christmas Eve is a central part of Brazilian celebrations, symbolizing the spiritual importance of the holiday. *Inspiration*: Consider attending a Midnight Mass or gathering with family for a reflective evening of carols and candlelight.
- *Ceia de Natal (Christmas Dinner)*: This meal is typically served after Mass and includes dishes like turkey, rice with raisins, and farofa (toasted cassava flour mixture). *Inspiration*: Try adding a

Brazilian dish such as farofa or a tropical fruit dessert like rabanada (Brazilian-style French toast) to your Christmas dinner.

Asian Christmas Traditions

6. The Philippines: The Longest Christmas Season The Philippines is known for celebrating the longest Christmas season, starting as early as September.

- *Simbang Gabi*: This nine-day series of dawn masses leading up to Christmas Eve is a cherished tradition. The last mass, Misa de Gallo, is celebrated at midnight. *Inspiration*: Incorporate early morning or late-night services into your holiday traditions to honor the Filipino spirit of devotion.
- *Parol Lanterns*: These star-shaped lanterns symbolize the Star of Bethlehem and are hung outside homes and churches. *Inspiration*: Craft parol lanterns with your family using bamboo sticks, colored paper, and lights for a colorful and meaningful decoration.

7. Japan: A Unique Take on Christmas Though Christmas in Japan is not a religious holiday, it has become a joyful occasion filled with unique customs.

- *Christmas Eve as a Romantic Holiday*: In Japan, Christmas Eve is akin to Valentine's Day, where couples celebrate with romantic dinners and exchange gifts. *Inspiration*: Dedicate Christmas Eve as a night for couples to enjoy a special dinner, exchanging heartfelt gifts and reflecting on the year.
- *KFC Christmas Dinner*: A quirky yet popular tradition in Japan is enjoying KFC on Christmas, started by a successful marketing campaign in the 1970s. *Inspiration*: Consider adding a humorous twist to your Christmas Eve dinner with fried chicken or creating your own fast-food-inspired feast at home.

African Christmas Traditions

8. South Africa: Summer Celebrations Christmas in South Africa falls during the summer, making outdoor activities and barbecues (braais) common.

- *Carols by Candlelight*: South Africans often gather outdoors for candlelight carol services that create a sense of community and celebration. *Inspiration*: Host an outdoor caroling session with friends and family, complete with handheld candles and summer refreshments.
- *Braai and Festive Dishes*: A Christmas braai might include meats, salads, and traditional desserts like Malva pudding (a spongy, caramelized pudding). *Inspiration*: Incorporate a few South African dishes into your holiday menu or hold an outdoor barbecue for a relaxed and festive Christmas meal.

9. Ethiopia: Timkat and Traditional Attire Ethiopia celebrates Christmas (Genna) on January 7, according to the Ethiopian Orthodox calendar.

- *Traditional Processions*: Celebrations include processions with people wearing traditional white clothing and playing drums and other instruments. *Inspiration*: Learn about Ethiopian culture by trying their traditional foods, such as injera (a sourdough flatbread) served with doro wat (spicy chicken stew).
- *Religious Significance*: Genna is a time for reflection, prayer, and community. It often includes festive sports like Genna, a game similar to field hockey. *Inspiration*: Integrate a friendly outdoor game into your holiday activities or set aside time for community service as a way to celebrate togetherness.

Integrating Global Traditions Into Your Christmas
1. Multicultural Decorations

- *Incorporate Diverse Elements*: Hang parol lanterns, display German nutcrackers, and use Mexican piñatas as festive decor.
- *Handmade Ornaments*: Create DIY ornaments inspired by global traditions, such as Swedish straw goats or German paper stars.

2. Food and Drink

- *Global Feast*: Plan a holiday meal that features dishes from different countries, allowing guests to experience various flavors.
- *Desserts from Around the World*: Try baking cookies from different cultures, such as Italian pizzelle, German stollen, or Polish pierniki (spiced cookies).

3. Music and Entertainment

- *Play Christmas Carols from Around the World*: Curate a playlist featuring holiday music from different cultures to set an international festive mood.
- *International Storytelling*: Read stories or folktales that explain how Christmas is celebrated in various cultures. This is a great activity for families with children.

4. Cultural Gift Ideas

- *Give Thoughtful, Culturally-Inspired Gifts*: Choose gifts that represent global traditions, such as handmade items from different countries, international food baskets, or cultural artifacts.

- *Charitable Giving*: Donate to charities that support causes in different parts of the world as a meaningful way to celebrate global togetherness.

Final Thoughts: A Global Celebration

Christmas is a season of unity and joy that transcends borders and beliefs. By incorporating global traditions into your celebrations, you not only expand your understanding of the holiday but also create a richer, more inclusive experience. Whether through food, decorations, music, or rituals, integrating elements from different cultures allows you to connect with the universal themes of love, generosity, and community that Christmas embodies. Embrace the diversity of the season, and let your holiday be a reflection of the world's shared spirit of festivity.

Chapter 14: Giving Back – Making Christmas Count for Others

Ideas for Community Service, Charity, and Meaningful Ways to Give Back During the Holiday Season

The true spirit of Christmas extends beyond the festive lights, gifts, and gatherings; it embodies generosity, compassion, and kindness. During the holiday season, giving back to the community and those in need can create profound and lasting impacts—not just for the recipients, but for those who give as well. Acts of service during this time foster gratitude, strengthen community bonds, and remind us that the greatest gifts we can share are time, love, and support. This chapter explores various ways to give back during the holiday season, providing inspiration for meaningful community service and charitable activities that make Christmas count for others.

The Importance of Giving Back During the Holidays

The holidays can be a time of joy and warmth for many, but for those facing financial difficulties, loneliness, or other challenges, it can be a difficult time. Engaging in community service and charitable activities not only helps alleviate the burdens of others but also enriches our own holiday experience by fostering empathy and connection.

Ideas for Community Service During the Holiday Season

1. Volunteering at Shelters and Food Banks

- *Serve Meals*: Volunteer to serve meals at local shelters or soup kitchens. Many community centers host special holiday dinners where volunteers are needed to prepare, serve, and clean up.
- *Organize Food Drives*: Collaborate with friends, neighbors, or colleagues to collect non-perishable food items and donate them

to local food banks. Consider including holiday staples like canned vegetables, stuffing mix, and dessert ingredients.

- *Meal Kits*: Create holiday meal kits with all the essentials a family might need for a special Christmas dinner. Include items like canned goods, pasta, sauce, rice, and a small dessert.

2. Collecting and Distributing Warm Clothing

- *Winter Clothing Drive*: Organize a drive to collect gently used or new coats, scarves, gloves, and hats. Distribute these items to homeless shelters or organizations that support low-income families.
- *Blanket Donations*: Collect or make warm blankets to donate to shelters or elderly care homes. Personalized blankets with holiday messages can add a comforting touch.
- *Socks and Warmers*: Socks are one of the most requested items at shelters. Pair socks with hand warmers for a small but impactful gift.

3. Helping Local Schools and Libraries

- *Reading to Children*: Volunteer to read holiday stories at local libraries or schools. This not only entertains but also fosters a love for reading among young audiences.
- *Holiday Craft Workshops*: Host or volunteer at holiday craft workshops where children can make their own Christmas decorations or gifts. This is a great way to engage with children and give parents a break.
- *Supply Donations*: Donate school supplies, books, or educational games to underfunded schools. Consider making a holiday-themed delivery with festive wrapping to add a touch of joy.

4. Supporting Animal Shelters

- *Pet Food Drive*: Organize a collection of pet food, toys, and bedding for local animal shelters. The holiday season often brings increased demand for shelter resources.
- *Volunteer Time*: Spend time at the shelter helping to walk dogs, play with cats, or assist with cleaning and feeding. Animals in shelters benefit from human interaction, which can improve their chances of adoption.
- *Adoption Sponsorship*: If possible, sponsor the adoption fee for a pet in need. This small gesture can help an animal find a loving home faster.

Charitable Activities for Individuals and Families
5. Participating in Gift-Giving Programs

- *Angel Tree Programs*: Participate in programs like the Salvation Army's Angel Tree, which provides children and families in need with personalized gifts. Choose a name or wish list, shop for the items, and return them wrapped and labeled.
- *Adopt-a-Family*: Partner with local charities to adopt a family for Christmas. Provide gifts, a holiday meal, and essentials like toiletries and household supplies to make their holiday brighter.
- *Operation Christmas Child*: Fill shoeboxes with small toys, school supplies, hygiene items, and notes of encouragement to be sent to children in need around the world.

6. DIY Care Packages

- *For the Homeless*: Assemble care packages with essentials such as toothbrushes, toothpaste, travel-sized toiletries, socks, snacks, and water bottles. Include a small holiday card with a message of hope.
- *For Seniors*: Create care packages with cozy items like slippers, tea bags, crossword puzzles, and a handwritten note. Deliver these to nursing homes or through programs that support elderly individuals who live alone.
- *For Healthcare Workers*: Show appreciation for healthcare workers by delivering care packages with snacks, energy bars, hand lotion, and handwritten thank-you notes. This gesture acknowledges their hard work, especially during the holiday season.

7. Donating Blood

- *Host a Blood Drive*: Partner with a local blood bank or hospital to organize a blood drive in your community or workplace.
- *Individual Donations*: If hosting isn't an option, schedule a time to donate blood yourself. Blood supplies often run low during the holidays, making this a simple yet life-saving act of service.

Innovative and Creative Ways to Give Back
8. Pay It Forward

- *Secret Acts of Kindness*: Pay for the coffee or meal of the person behind you in line. Small acts like these can create a ripple effect of kindness in your community.
- *Holiday Cards for Strangers*: Leave holiday cards with uplifting messages in public places like libraries, park benches, or community bulletin boards for strangers to find and enjoy.

- *Gift Cards for Essentials*: Leave gift cards for grocery stores, pharmacies, or local shops in strategic places where someone in need might find them.

9. Virtual Volunteering

- *Online Tutoring*: Offer tutoring or homework help for children through virtual platforms. This is especially valuable for students who might be struggling academically due to remote learning challenges.
- *Phone Calls to Seniors*: Reach out to local senior centers to volunteer for phone calls or video chats with elderly residents who may feel isolated during the holidays.
- *Digital Fundraising*: Host a virtual charity event, such as a Christmas-themed trivia night or online auction, with proceeds going to a chosen charity.

10. Holiday Fundraisers

- *Bake Sales for Charity*: Organize a holiday bake sale with proceeds going to local charities. Include festive treats like gingerbread cookies, cinnamon rolls, and fruitcakes.
- *Charity Runs*: Participate in or organize a "Santa Run" or a holiday-themed charity walk/run where participants dress up in festive attire, with entry fees donated to a cause.
- *Craft Sales*: Sell homemade holiday crafts such as ornaments, wreaths, or decorations and donate the profits to a local organization.

Inspiring Ways for Children and Families to Give Back
11. Teaching Kids the Joy of Giving

- *Toy Donations*: Encourage children to choose gently used toys they no longer play with and donate them to a local children's hospital or shelter.
- *Cookie Delivery*: Spend an afternoon baking cookies as a family, then deliver them to neighbors, teachers, or local fire and police stations to show appreciation.
- *Holiday Story Swap*: Organize a virtual or in-person storytelling session where children read or tell stories to other kids, especially those who may not have family close by.

12. Family Volunteer Projects

- *Community Cleanup*: Spend a day cleaning up a local park or playground as a family. Bring holiday-themed garbage bags and gloves to make it fun and engaging.
- *Soup Kitchen Shifts*: Volunteer together at a soup kitchen. This experience teaches children compassion and the value of helping others.
- *Decorating Community Spaces*: Work with local community centers or nursing homes to decorate common areas with holiday cheer. This act brings joy to spaces that may otherwise feel sterile or forgotten.

Making Charitable Giving Part of Your Holiday Tradition

13. Set Up a Family Giving Jar Create a jar where family members can contribute spare change throughout the year. In December, decide together how to use the funds—whether donating to a charity, buying groceries for a family in need, or sponsoring holiday gifts for children.

14. Pledge Time, Not Just Money If monetary donations are not feasible, commit to giving time. Offer to run errands for an elderly neighbor, shovel snow for someone unable to do so, or babysit for a single parent so they can shop for gifts or relax.

15. Involve the Workplace or School

- *Group Volunteer Day*: Organize a group volunteer day with colleagues or school classmates. This could involve sorting donations, wrapping gifts for charity, or distributing food at a food bank.
- *Holiday Charity Drive*: Coordinate a drive where coworkers or students contribute items such as canned goods, winter clothing, or toys. Incentivize participation with friendly competitions or rewards.

Final Thoughts: Making Christmas Count for Others

The holiday season provides a perfect opportunity to reflect on what it means to give. Whether it's through time, effort, or resources, giving back allows us to create moments of hope and joy for those who need it most. By incorporating community service, charitable activities, and acts of kindness into your Christmas traditions, you can spread the warmth of the season beyond your immediate circle and make a positive difference. Let this holiday be a reminder that the greatest gifts we can offer are those that come from the heart—time, love, and kindness.

Chapter 15: Preparing for a New Year with Gratitude
Reflections on the Season, Tips on Concluding Holiday Celebrations with a Grateful Heart, and Looking Ahead to the New Year

As the holiday season draws to a close, it's natural to reflect on the moments shared with loved ones, the acts of kindness experienced and given, and the sense of warmth that filled your home. The transition from Christmas to the New Year provides an opportunity to pause, take stock, and embrace gratitude for the past while setting intentions for what lies ahead. Concluding your holiday celebrations with a grateful heart not only enhances the joy of the season but also sets the foundation for a positive and mindful start to the New Year. This chapter explores how to reflect meaningfully on the holiday season, cultivate gratitude, and prepare for the year to come.

The Importance of Reflecting on the Holiday Season

The holiday season is often a whirlwind of activity, filled with laughter, meals, gifts, and gatherings. Once the festivities wind down, taking time to reflect helps us process the experiences and appreciate the moments that truly mattered. Reflecting with intention allows you to:

- Recognize and savor moments of joy and connection.
- Acknowledge the efforts of those who contributed to the season's warmth.
- Understand how holiday experiences have impacted your sense of gratitude and well-being.

Tips for Concluding Holiday Celebrations with Gratitude
1. Create a Gratitude Ritual

- *Daily Gratitude Journal*: Start or continue a gratitude journal where you record moments from the holiday season that brought joy, peace, or love. This could include small things like a spontaneous laugh with a friend or a particularly delicious meal shared with family.
- *Family Gratitude Circle*: Gather family members for a post-holiday reflection where each person shares what they're most thankful for from the season. This practice can strengthen bonds and offer different perspectives on shared moments.
- *Morning or Evening Reflection*: Dedicate time in the morning or evening to sit quietly and reflect on the holiday memories that brought you the most happiness. Close your eyes, breathe deeply, and allow yourself to relive those moments in detail.

2. Send Thank-You Notes

- *Personalized Notes*: Write and send thank-you notes to people who made your holiday special, such as friends who hosted gatherings, family members who prepared meals, or colleagues who shared gifts or warm wishes. This simple act not only spreads gratitude but also reinforces connections.
- *Digital Appreciation*: If mailing notes isn't feasible, send heartfelt messages through email or text. Include specific details about what you appreciated to make your gratitude feel more genuine and impactful.

3. Reflect Through Photos and Keepsakes

- *Photo Album Creation*: Assemble a physical or digital photo album that captures the highlights of your holiday season. Include captions or notes detailing why each moment was meaningful.
- *Memory Box*: Create a holiday memory box to store cards, notes, small gifts, or decorations that have special significance. Revisiting this box in future years can help relive cherished moments and strengthen feelings of gratitude.
- *Slideshow Recap*: Gather with friends or family to watch a slideshow of photos and videos from the holidays. Pair this with a cozy evening and warm drinks for an enjoyable and reflective way to conclude the season.

Mindful Decluttering and Letting Go

Concluding the holiday season also means transitioning your space and mindset into the New Year. Decluttering with intention can symbolize a fresh start and help you focus on what truly matters.

1. Declutter Holiday Decor with Gratitude

- *Mindful Packing*: As you take down decorations, reflect on the memories attached to each item. Say a quiet "thank you" for the joy they brought to your holiday before carefully storing them.
- *Donate Excess*: If you find decorations or gifts that no longer serve you, consider donating them to a charity or community center. This practice helps pass on the joy they once brought you to others.
- *Create a Holiday Inventory*: As you pack away your holiday items, make a note of what you have and what you may not need in the future. This helps with more mindful planning next year and reduces clutter.

2. Refresh Your Space

- *Deep Clean and Organize*: Use the time after the holidays to clean your home and rearrange items to create a sense of newness. Clear out spaces that were cluttered during holiday gatherings to set a fresh, peaceful tone for the New Year.
- *Incorporate Nature*: Bring elements of nature into your home to maintain warmth and tranquility. Replace holiday greenery with houseplants, branches, or winter flowers to keep the spirit of comfort alive.
- *Reflective Decor*: Choose home decorations that inspire calm and positivity, such as framed quotes about gratitude or items that evoke happy memories.

Looking Ahead to the New Year

Starting the New Year with gratitude can significantly impact how you approach new goals, challenges, and opportunities. By carrying the sense of fulfillment from the holiday season into the New Year, you create a positive foundation for growth and mindfulness.

1. Set Intentions, Not Just Resolutions

- *Intention Setting*: Rather than focusing solely on resolutions that may feel daunting, set intentions that emphasize positive actions and attitudes. For example, "I intend to be more patient" or "I intend to spend more quality time with loved ones."
- *Vision Board*: Create a vision board with images, words, and symbols that represent what you hope to achieve or experience in the coming year. This can serve as a daily reminder of your intentions and help keep your focus aligned.

2. Reflect on Lessons Learned

- *Holiday Takeaways*: Think about what you learned from this holiday season. Did you realize the importance of slowing down? Did you learn that simplifying gift-giving brought more joy? Use these reflections to guide how you approach future holiday seasons and the New Year.
- *Challenges and Growth*: Acknowledge any difficulties or stressful moments you faced and identify how you overcame them or what you can learn from them. Gratitude isn't just about positive experiences; it's also about recognizing resilience and growth.

3. Gratitude-Fueled Goal Setting

- *Gratitude as a Foundation*: When setting goals, start by listing things you're already grateful for. This can shift your mindset from focusing on lack to appreciating abundance, making your goals feel like an extension of what you already have.
- *Gratitude Journal Continuation*: Carry forward your gratitude journal practice into the New Year. Writing down three things you're grateful for each day can increase mindfulness, improve mood, and reinforce a positive outlook.

4. Acts of Service and Continued Giving

- *Plan Community Service*: Keep the spirit of giving alive by planning community service activities throughout the New Year. This could be volunteering at a local shelter, participating in community clean-ups, or organizing charity drives.
- *Monthly Acts of Kindness*: Incorporate a habit of performing monthly acts of kindness, such as writing appreciation notes to friends, helping a neighbor, or making a small donation to a cause that resonates with you.

Creating Traditions That Foster Gratitude

Incorporating gratitude-focused traditions into your holiday season and beyond can make the end of the year feel more meaningful and create lasting habits that enrich your life.

1. The Gratitude Jar

- *How It Works*: Throughout the holiday season and into the New Year, write down moments you're thankful for on small pieces of paper and place them in a jar. At the end of the year, open the jar and reflect on those moments as a family or individually.
- *Family Tradition*: Make this a recurring practice that encourages all family members to contribute, fostering a shared culture of gratitude.

2. End-of-Year Gratitude Dinner

- *A Special Meal*: Host a dinner on New Year's Eve or New Year's Day where everyone shares something they are grateful for from the past year. This can become a cherished tradition that closes out the holiday season with warmth and reflection.
- *Candle Lighting Ceremony*: Include a candle-lighting ceremony where each person lights a candle as they share their moment of gratitude. This adds a symbolic act of bringing light and positivity into the New Year.

Final Thoughts: Embracing the New Year with an Open Heart

The holiday season may come and go, but the lessons and memories it brings can linger throughout the New Year. By ending the season with gratitude and mindful reflection, you carry the warmth of Christmas into the coming months, setting a tone of positivity, empathy, and hope. Whether through personal reflection, new traditions, or acts of kindness, embracing gratitude enriches your life and the lives of those around you. Let this season of giving inspire you to step into the New Year with an open heart, ready to cherish each moment and make every day count.

<u>Message from the Author:</u>

I hope you enjoyed this book, I love astrology and knew there was not a book such as this out on the shelf. I love metaphysical items as well. Please check out my other books:

-Life of Government Benefits

-My life of Hell

-My life with Hydrocephalus

-Red Sky

-World Domination:Woman's rule

-World Domination:Woman's Rule 2: The War

-Life and Banishment of Apophis: book 1

-The Kidney Friendly Diet

-The Ultimate Hemp Cookbook

-Creating a Dispensary(legally)

-Cleanliness throughout life: the importance of showering from childhood to adulthood.

-Strong Roots: The Risks of Overcoddling children

-Hemp Horoscopes: Cosmic Insights and Earthly Healing

- Celestial Hemp Navigating the Zodiac: Through the Green Cosmos

-Astrological Hemp: Aligning The Stars with Earth's Ancient Herb

-The Astrological Guide to Hemp: Stars, Signs, and Sacred Leaves

-Green Growth: Innovative Marketing Strategies for your Hemp Products and Dispensary

-Cosmic Cannabis

-Astrological Munchies

-Henry The Hemp

-Zodiacal Roots: The Astrological Soul Of Hemp

- Green Constellations: Intersection of Hemp and Zodiac

-Hemp in The Houses: An astrological Adventure Through The Cannabis Galaxy

-Galactic Ganja Guide

Heavenly Hemp

Zodiac Leaves

Doctor Who Astrology

Cannastrology

Stellar Satvias and Cosmic Indicas

Celestial Cannabis: A Zodiac Journey

AstroHerbology: The Sky and The Soil: Volume 1

AstroHerbology:Celestial Cannabis:Volume 2

Cosmic Cannabis Cultivation

The Starry Guide to Herbal Harmony: Volume 1

The Starry Guide to Herbal Harmony: Cannabis Universe: Volume 2

Yugioh Astrology: Astrological Guide to Deck, Duels and more

Nightmare Mansion: Echoes of The Abyss

Nightmare Mansion 2: Legacy of Shadows

Nightmare Mansion 3: Shadows of the Forgotten

Nightmare Mansion 4: Echoes of the Damned

The Life and Banishment of Apophis: Book 2

Nightmare Mansion: Halls of Despair

Healing with Herb: Cannabis and Hydrocephalus

Planetary Pot: Aligning with Astrological Herbs: Volume 1

Fast Track to Freedom: 30 Days to Financial Independence Using AI, Assets, and Agile Hustles

Cosmic Hemp Pathways

How to Become Financially Free in 30 Days: 10,000 Paths to Prosperity

Zodiacal Herbage: Astrological Insights: Volume 1
Nightmare Mansion: Whispers in the Walls
The Daleks Invade Atlantis
Henry the hemp and Hydrocephalus

10X The Kidney Friendly Diet
Cannabis Universe: Adult coloring book
Hemp Astrology: The Healing Power of the Stars
Zodiacal Herbage: Astrological Insights: Cannabis Universe: Volume 2
<u>**Planetary Pot: Aligning with Astrological Herbs: Cannabis Universes: Volume 2**</u>
Doctor Who Meets the Replicators and SG-1: The Ultimate Battle for Survival
Nightmare Mansion: Curse of the Blood Moon
<u>**The Celestial Stoner: A Guide to the Zodiac**</u>
Cosmic Pleasures: Sex Toy Astrology for Every Sign
Hydrocephalus Astrology: Navigating the Stars and Healing Waters
Lapis and the Mischievous Chocolate Bar

Celestial Positions: Sexual Astrology for Every Sign
Apophis's Shadow Work Journal: : A Journey of Self-Discovery and Healing
Kinky Cosmos: Sexual Kink Astrology for Every Sign
Digital Cosmos: The Astrological Digimon Compendium
Stellar Seeds: The Cosmic Guide to Growing with Astrology
Apophis's Daily Gratitude Journal

Cat Astrology: Feline Mysteries of the Cosmos
The Cosmic Kama Sutra: An Astrological Guide to Sexual Positions
Unleash Your Potential: A Guided Journal Powered by AI Insights

Whispers of the Enchanted Grove

Cosmic Pleasures: An Astrological Guide to Sexual Kinks
369, 12 Manifestation Journal
Whisper of the nocturne journal(blank journal for writing or drawing)
The Boogey Book
Locked In Reflection: A Chastity Journey Through Locktober
Generating Wealth Quickly:
How to Generate $100,000 in 24 Hours
Star Magic: Harness the Power of the Universe
The Flatulence Chronicles: A Fart Journal for Self-Discovery
The Doctor and The Death Moth
Seize the Day: A Personal Seizure Tracking Journal
The Ultimate Boogeyman Safari: A Journey into the Boogie World and Beyond
Whispers of Samhain: 1,000 Spells of Love, Luck, and Lunar Magic: Samhain Spell Book
Apophis's guides:
Witch's Spellbook Crafting Guide for Halloween
<u>Frost & Flame: The Enchanted Yule Grimoire of 1000 Winter Spells</u>
<u>The Ultimate Boogey Goo Guide & Spooky Activities for Halloween Fun</u>
Harmony of the Scales: A Libra's Spellcraft for Balance and Beauty
The Enchanted Advent: 36 Days of Christmas Wonders

Nightmare Mansion: The Labyrinth of Screams
Harvest of Enchantment: 1,000 Spells of Gratitude, Love, and Fortune for Thanksgiving
The Boogey Chronicles: A Journal of Nightly Encounters and Shadowy Secrets

The 12 Days of Financial Freedom: A Step-by-Step Christmas Countdown to Transform Your Finances

Sigil of the Eternal Spiral Blank Journal

A Christmas Feast: Timeless Recipes for Every Meal

Holiday Stress-Free Solutions: A Survival Guide to Thriving During the Festive Season

Yu-Gi-Oh! Holiday Gifting Mastery: The Ultimate Guide for Fans and Newcomers Alike

Holiday Harmony: A Hydrocephalus Survival Guide for the Festive Season

Celestial Craft: The Witch's Almanac for 2025 – A Cosmic Guide to Manifestations, Moons, and Mystical Events

Doctor Who: The Toymaker's Winter Wonderland

Tulsa King Unveiled: A Thrilling Guide to Stallone's Mafia Masterpiece

Pendulum Craft: A Complete Guide to Crafting and Using Personalized Divination Tools

Nightmare Mansion: Santa's Eternal Eve

Starlight Noel: A Cosmic Journey through Christmas Mysteries

The Dark Architect: Unlocking the Blueprint of Existence

Surviving the Embrace: The Ultimate Guide to Encounters with The Hugging Molly

The Enchanted Codex: Secrets of the Craft for Witches, Wiccans, and Pagans

Harvest of Gratitude: A Complete Thanksgiving Guide

If you want solar for your home go here: https://www.harborso-lar.live/apophisenterprises/

Get Some Tarot cards: https://www.makeplayingcards.com/sell/ apophis-occult-shop

Get some shirts: https://www.bonfire.com/store/apophis-shirt-emporium/

<u>Instagrams:</u>
@apophis_enterprises,
@apophisbookemporium,
@apophisscardshop
Twitter: @apophisenterpr1
 Tiktok:@apophisenterprise
Youtube: @sg1fan23477, @FiresideRetreatKingdom
Hive: @sg1fan23477
CheeLee: @SG1fan23477

Podcast: Apophis Chat Zone: https://open.spotify.com/show/5zXbrCLEV2xzCp8ybrfHsk?si=fb4d4fdbdce44dec

Newsletter: https://apophiss-newsletter-27c897.beehiiv.com/

www.ingramcontent.com/pod-product-compliance
Lightning Source LLC
Chambersburg PA
CBHW072101150726
47999CB00005B/1828